Woman of Worth is insightful, challenging, a brilliant new twist on this familiar chapter of Scripture, and an excellent resource for small group or individual study.

Mary Lenaburg, *speaker and author of* ***Be Brave in the Scared***

The ancient woman profiled in Proverbs 31 continues to provoke debate and discussion. How much of her life is applicable to today's woman? The answer is: all of it! Melanie Rigney unpacks these verses with sensitivity and realistic thinking, coupled with a desire to live a full life in service to God and others.

Pat Gohn, *author of* ***Blest, Beautiful, and Bodacio***
Celebrating the Gift of Catholic Womanhood

Woman of Worth is definitely worth reading as w...
each day in the midst of the daily pressures and demands that take a toll on our self-worth.

Carol Monaco, *author of* ***Treasures of the Rosary*** *and* ***Heavenly Mother Help Me***

Melanie powerfully unpacks Proverbs to help us make a beautiful life from what we already have and to celebrate our divine daughterhood in the midst of our busy-ness.

Rose Folsom, *author at VirtueConnection.com*

Melanie not only explains what the Proverbs gal was up to, she makes her seem real and someone to admire and hopefully emulate even if we do it in different ways.

Patricia Lorenz, *29-year* ***Daily Guideposts*** *contributor*
and author of fourteen books

Having just weathered a financial crisis in my marriage, I was struck by Melanie's suggestion that self-worth bolstered by a respectful partnership is the kind of "income that matters." Her words offered healing for a painful episode in my life.

Pam Spano, *Being Catholic… Really, CatholicMom.com,*
and Catholic365.com writer

Who doesn't have broken places in their life? Melanie Rigney astutely guides women through Proverbs 31, opening their minds and hearts to their own magnificent value.

ALLISON GINGRAS, *author of* ***The Stay Connected Journals for Catholic Women***

A mini-retreat/spring cleaning for the soul to help determine what needs to stay and what needs to go in order to put God first in our lives.

MARY SHEA, *freelance writer, Washington, DC*

These stories and reflections, especially the way Melanie tells them, speak directly to each one of us seeking to find how we are women of worth.

JOAN SHEPPARD, *Director of Faith Formation, Good Shepherd Catholic Church, Alexandria, VA*

This book reminded me that my efforts, my weaknesses, my small attempts, and my love for the Lord are "enough."

LAUREN PUZDER, *Bristow, VA*

Practical advice that will engage and sustain its readers, these chapters provide a constructive bridge from Proverbs to reality.

PATRICIA WATSON, *Executive Assistant, Landings International*

Each chapter contains so many images and insights to ponder, savor, and apply to your own life as a woman of worth.

CHRISTINE MARIE EBERLE, *author of* ***Finding God in Ordinary Time***

Melanie increases our awareness of how each of us can bring to life this ideal woman of worth from within.

MARY LOU SWANBERG, *Life Line Counseling 4 Addictions, Warrenton, VA*

Melanie Rigney is the real deal! Authentic, down to earth, yet awe inspiring. She knows well the qualities she writes about in *Women of Worth* because she lives them.

NANCY HC WARD, *author, editor, and speaker*

WOMAN *of* WORTH

PRAYERS AND **REFLECTIONS** FOR **WOMEN INSPIRED** BY THE **BOOK** OF **PROVERBS**

MELANIE RIGNEY

To **Duffy Kiko** & **Mary Ellen Gilroy**,

sisters in Christ and women of worth

Twenty-Third Publications
One Montauk Avenue, Suite 200
New London, CT 06320
(860) 437-3012 or (800) 321-0411
www.twentythirdpublications.com

Cover image: iStockphoto.com / marabird

ISBN: 978-1-62785-338-5
Library of Congress Control Number: 2018962307
Printed in the U.S.A.

CONTENTS

Who can find a woman of worth?
    Far beyond jewels is her value.
Her husband trusts her judgment;
    he does not lack income.
She brings him profit, not loss,
    all the days of her life.
She seeks out wool and flax
    and weaves with skillful hands.
Like a merchant fleet,
    she secures her provisions from afar.
She rises while it is still night,
    and distributes food to her household,
    a portion to her maidservants.
She picks out a field and acquires it;
    from her earnings she plants a vineyard.
She girds herself with strength;
    she exerts her arms with vigor.
She enjoys the profit from her dealings;
    her lamp is never extinguished at night.
She puts her hands to the distaff,
    and her fingers ply the spindle.
She reaches out her hands to the poor,
    and extends her arms to the needy.

She is not concerned for her household when it snows—
all her charges are doubly clothed.
She makes her own coverlets;
fine linen and purple are her clothing.
Her husband is prominent at the city gates
as he sits with the elders of the land.
She makes garments and sells them,
and stocks the merchants with belts.
She is clothed with strength and dignity,
and laughs at the days to come.
She opens her mouth in wisdom;
kindly instruction is on her tongue.
She watches over the affairs of her household,
and does not eat the bread of idleness.
Her children rise up and call her blessed;
her husband, too, praises her:
"Many are the women of proven worth,
but you have excelled them all."
Charm is deceptive and beauty fleeting;
the woman who fears the Lord is to be praised.
Acclaim her for the work of her hands,
and let her deeds praise her at the city gates.

Proverbs 31:10–31

INTRODUCTION

Who can find a woman of worth?
Far beyond jewels is her value.

Proverbs 31:10

I have a confession. This book was born out of anger.

A good friend, an acquaintance, and I were talking about Proverbs 31's poem on the woman of worth. Acquaintance said it set an impossible standard for wives and mothers. It was not the first time she had expressed her view that childless single women have it easy. Good Friend and I allowed as how we'd been to an eightieth birthday party the week before and while the birthday girl wasn't perfect, she exemplified the women of worth's traits. Acquaintance said the birthday girl must not have children. I noted that she has eight of them and numerous grandchildren, and anyway, I thought the passage was not only about women with children, but also about Christ and his church and our individual relationships with the Lord.

"Oh," Acquaintance all but oozed, "you're thinking of it *metaphorically*."

"Ain't nothing metaphoric about my relationship with Jesus," I shot back.

Crickets.

I felt bad the whole way home for having lost my temper. Then I started thinking: maybe it was progress that I thought my relationship with Jesus *did* make me a woman of worth. For most of my life, I downplayed any accomplishments or compliments. Nothing I did was really that important; anything I could do, someone else could do better.

I delved a bit further into Proverbs 31 and learned that it was long believed that King Lemuel, whose mother gave him this instruction, was Solomon, which would make his mother Bathsheba. You know, Bathsheba, the woman with whom King David had sex and then sent her husband off to death in battle to hide that Bathsheba was pregnant. That child died shortly after birth, but the couple went on to have Solomon. We don't know for sure that Lemuel and Solomon are the same person, but I really like the idea of Bathsheba, someone familiar with sin and tragedy and forgiveness, holding forth on the attributes of a worthy woman.

So, here we are. Thanks, God.

Each chapter in this book includes a verse or two from Proverbs 31. In addition to a short narrative, you'll find reflections on two words from the verse's essence, a brief profile of a woman saint who exemplifies the verse, three questions for contemplation or discussion, and a prayer. Start at the beginning, or pick a verse that speaks to where you are today.

My prayer is that something in this book will speak to your heart and soul and further open them to the Lord. He loves you very much. Know that in his eyes, you indeed are a woman of worth.

CHAPTER 1

OF TRUST *and* JUDGMENT

Her husband trusts her judgment; he does not lack income.

Proverbs 31:11

As my twenty-year marriage neared its end, my husband and I had more than $200,000 in credit card debt. Most of it was in my name since I was the primary income earner—or had been, until I'd been fired a few months earlier. We were sitting in our family room one day, arguing for the umpteenth time about the future, when he said, "You don't believe in me anymore."

He was right. And that, more than the debt or anything else, spelled the end of the marriage. I hadn't believed in him or trusted his judgment for some time; to me, he'd become a drain, a burden. It was a far cry from the place we'd begun, both ambitious journalists, born and raised in the Midwest, our future together full of promise because we had the same political views and liked the same music. That God thing? Didn't matter. Neither of us ever went to church, and we'd been married by a justice of the peace.

TRUST

I think about the marriages I admire among my friends today. It's not that the unions are perfect, and in some cases, to the outside world, they don't appear evenly yoked. There are big differences in age or background or education or political persuasion in many. Sometimes, they aren't from the same faiths. What they do have in common is that trust and respect for each other's judgment mentioned in Proverbs 31:11. Maybe he's not Catholic, but he respects her devotion to her faith. It makes her stronger and more loving (and perhaps, leads to unconscious evangelization opportunities). Maybe he at one point worked erratic or long hours that kept him away from important family functions. Her wisdom in selecting the times to discuss if or how that might change instead of erupting into tears or shouts every time he got home late resulted in small but important changes to his schedule even though the adjustments had a negative impact on his promotion possibilities.

That sort of trust gets people through the rough spots where some might regard them as lacking income—the dollars and cents kind—because they have the income that matters. That income is a sense of safety, confidence, and self-worth bolstered by a respectful partnership.

As women of worth, we attempt to be worthy of that trust in all our relationships: with spouses, with children and other relatives, with friends, with neighbors and coworkers, and with the Lord. When we have people we can trust and who can trust us, we all go about our daily work with less fear and uncertainty.

What about those times when trust is betrayed or disregarded—by us, by others, and, so it seems, by God? It's when our spouse is caught in a lie—or is caught setting traps or scrutinizing our habits in search of a lie—that distance begins to open up; we read Proverbs 31:11 and the rest of the woman of worth passage and shake our heads. No earthly woman has that kind of relationship with anyone. But we can. It's there for the asking with the Lord.

Throughout the Bible, we are told to trust in the Lord, not humankind, over and over again. But in Numbers 12:7–8, God notes that while he speaks with prophets through visions and dreams, it's different with Moses, a human being:

> Throughout my house he is worthy of trust:
> face to face I speak to him,
> plainly and not in riddles.
> The likeness of the Lord he beholds.

What did Moses do to earn God's trust? He obeyed. He carried the Lord's messages to Pharaoh and the Israelites even when he knew he would be challenged, disbelieved, and scoffed at. He humbled himself. All laudable characteristics. All characteristics within our grasp, if we are willing to ask.

But instead of summoning up the courage and faith to ask, all too often we act as if we're in charge of the trust equation: Here's the deal, Lord. I'll go to Mass on Sundays and holidays, I'll give money to the parish, I'll get the kids or myself to religious ed or Bible study or prayer group, and you'll give me a life without worry in exchange. When the equation gets upset by infidelity, illness, poverty, or some other twist, we work to identify where our trust was misplaced. In our spouse? Make his life a living hell in retribution. In our children? Weep and wail to anyone who will listen. In ourselves? Find some refuge in alcohol, food, shopping, or other overindulgence as a means of self-punishment. In God? That's easy. Just turn our backs on him.

If we truly desire to be women of worth—of worth to the Lord, to the world, and to ourselves—we have to at some point begin to trust again, and again, and again. When Peter asked if he had to forgive a sinning brother seven times, Jesus's response was not seven times, but seventy times seven. We don't need to stay in situations that are dangerous to us or to those we love. Forgiveness can come from a distance as we prepare ourselves to discern when—if ever—the time comes to open up our hearts and souls to again trusting those who have wronged us, intentionally or unintentionally.

We find these beautiful words in the *Catechism of the Catholic Church* about reestablishing relationships within a marriage: "To heal the wounds of sin, man and woman need the help of the grace that God in his infinite mercy never refuses them" (CCC, 1608). That same infinite mercy is available to us in healing any rupture.

JUDGMENT

The woman of worth's husband trusted her judgment. That's a weighty responsibility, sisters. As women of worth, we are influential, whether we realize it or not. Our children, friends, coworkers, and people in the parish whose names we don't even know are watching us. They hope to learn from us. And so, we must judge carefully. Jesus tells us in Matthew 7:2, "For as you judge, so will you be judged, and the measure with which you measure will be measured out to you."

The woman of worth's judgment likely involved much observation: Who among her husband's business partners conducted themselves ethically. Who provided financially for their families, including aging relatives, and who was miserly with their wealth. Who was kind to the children, and whose children seemed uneasy at the community's gatherings. What the business partners' own wives said about the men when the women gathered for activities.

That sort of judgment isn't about liking or disliking someone for the tone of her voice or the color of her skin. It isn't about whether she's driving a ten-year-old car or wearing fashions from five years ago. It's about taking the measure of the person to prepare yourself to go into battle with or against her. Consider Jesus's observations of the authorities. He was slow to publicly condemn them, even when they were attempting to trap him in word games. He'd tell a story and listen and watch. Remember the story of the woman found in adultery? Jesus didn't dish a lot of dirt on the scribes and the Pharisees. Instead, when they asked him about whether she should be stoned, he wrote something on the ground and said the person without sin should cast the first stone. Quietly, the others left, having judged themselves.

The woman of worth was careful in her judging—of others and of herself. She wasn't constantly going to her husband and others talking about what a total loser she was. She believed in her own worth—and we are called to do the same, even when we stumble and fall. We all sin. But as Christians, we know it needn't end there. As Pope Francis said in his beautiful encyclical letter *Laudato Si'* in May 2015:

> Human beings, while capable of the worst, are also capable of rising above themselves, choosing again what is good, and making a new start, despite their mental and social conditioning. We are able to take an honest look at ourselves, to acknowledge our deep dissatisfaction, and to embark on new paths to authentic freedom.[1]

The woman of worth's honest, compassionate actions and words made her a trustworthy, reliable companion of great value for her spouse, her friends, her children, and the Lord.

1 http://w2.vatican.va/content/francesco/en/encyclicals/documents/papa-francesco_20150524_enciclica-laudato-si.html

A WOMAN OF WORTH

Blessed Chiara Badano

1971–1990 • Feast day – October 29

Chiara Badano never married and never had children before she died in October 1990. Her life was indistinguishable from that of many other Italian teenagers: She loved her parents, went to school, had friends, was active in a Christian movement called Focolare, and played sports. All that changed one day on the tennis court when the pretty seventeen-year-old suffered a pain so intense that she dropped her racquet. Tests showed that Chiara was suffering from bone cancer, and that a cure was unlikely.

Bitterness over the injustice of this diagnosis would have been understandable given Chiara's youth. But she chose to trust and love instead. She served as a source of comfort to the caregivers and friends who came to see her. One Valentine's Day, Chiara surprised her parents with news they would be spending the evening not in the hospital with her, but at a restaurant dinner she had arranged. When the pain of her treatments would seem almost unbearable, she would say, "For you, Jesus...if you want it, I want it too."[2]

Chiara was buried in the plain white dress she had selected; she regarded it as her wedding dress, as she would be united with Christ in heaven, confident in his judgment of her.

2 http://www.focolare.org/en/news/2012/10/29/beata-chiara-luce-badano/

FINDING YOUR WORTH

1. We all encounter difficult circumstances that can cause us to lose trust in the Lord, temporarily or for a more extended period. Those circumstances might include the sudden loss of loved ones, the end of a dream, or health issues. Where have you become bitter and vowed that when you get to heaven, the Lord is going to have some explaining to do? Make a pact with yourself and God that you will limit your thinking about this perceived injustice to thirty minutes a day, followed by fifteen minutes of offering thanks for the ways in which the Lord has blessed you.

2. Do you sometimes feel like God trusts you a little *too* much? Where are you feeling overwhelmed and overburdened in family roles, at work, and in ministry or friendships? Ask the Lord for some direction, and listen rather than coming up with reasons why the current path doesn't work for you. Consider talking with a priest or spiritual adviser if the Lord's way for you still seems a bit murky and challenging.

3. Is there someone who has lost your trust, perhaps for very legitimate reasons? Rather than nursing the hurt, in what ways might that trust begin to be rebuilt, without putting yourself in danger? Options might include sincerely praying for the person, or looking for small opportunities in which you can open yourself up.

Lord, help me to believe in your trust in me; to trust in you; and to build loving, trusting relationships with others.

CHAPTER 2

OF PROFIT *and* LOSS

She brings him profit, not loss, all the days of her life.
Proverbs 31:12

You know how it goes when a relationship begins. Whether it's the start of a romance or platonic friendship, we're on our best behavior. We put on makeup and take a little more care with our clothing and hair. We're patient, attentive, and compassionate.

Then, after a while, things get familiar. We complain when it's our husband's or roommate's turn to take out the recycling and it doesn't happen. We figure there's no need to fancy up. We start talking over or interrupting. When we stop bringing profit, or good, to the relationship, everyone loses.

The same can happen in our spiritual life. Seasons and sacraments and downright miracles remind us of the Lord's awesome love for us, and, having experienced them, we plan to spend more time in prayer, more time offering up spiritual and corporal works of mercy, more time just being kind and considerate. Then we get busy, and our best intentions fall by the wayside. Then we beat ourselves up for our perceived lack of devotion, which only distances us further from him. What's a gal to do to keep things fresh and exciting? Rethinking the equation as we perceive it can help.

PROFIT

The woman of worth sees profit as something other than dollars and cents and a balance sheet, and perhaps that is why some editions of the Bible use the words "good" and "harm" in place of "profit" and "loss" in Proverbs 31:12. Personally, I like the strength of profit and loss. Profit is something we seek to bring to—and receive from—all our human interactions when we are at our best. Children profit and learn from parents who provide loving guidance. Spouses profit and learn from mates whom they trust and respect. Friends profit and learn from those who listen more than they talk, and from whose advice and admonishments are offered sparingly and wisely.

St. Ignatius Loyola counsels us to consider times when we receive sharp words, when we are humbled, when we are called to practice charity, patience, and the like as "gain for you, and you should seek to procure them; and at the close of that day, you should go to rest most cheerful and pleased."[3]

Consider the spiritual works of mercy that involve actively giving or receiving correction: counseling the doubtful, instructing the ignorant, admonishing the sinner, and comforting the sorrowful. (The other three, forgiving injuries, bearing wrongs patiently, and praying for the living and the dead, do not necessarily involve navigating a conversation with someone else.) It's not easy to be on the giving or receiving end of any of these works. It's as hard to tell a friend with love that, after two years of unemployment, it is unlikely he will find a job at the salary to which he was accustomed, and to offer to help him simplify his lifestyle, as it is to hear that your fondness for wine is becoming a problem. But we profit when we have the courage to listen to those who desire to help us with our deficits, and when we have the courage to offer correction to others.

3 Assaf, Andrea Kirk. *The Saints' Little Book of Wisdom: The Essential Teachings*, p. 370.

I'm not thinking the woman of worth ran around and complained about her husband to her five best girlfriends. She brought him profit in that way, by going to him directly when she believed he was veering off the narrow path.

It's wonderful when we get through such conversations as adults and loving brothers and sisters in Christ. But what about the times that we take a stand and are ridiculed, shunned, or worse? There is profit in them as well. Indeed, in the Sermon on the Mount, Jesus counsels the crowds to "rejoice and be glad" when they are persecuted and reviled, "for your reward will be great in heaven. Thus they persecuted the prophets who were before you" (Matthew 5:12).

Some businesses make decisions based on short-term profits, the ones shareholders will see immediately in their stock portfolio or quarterly statements. It might make sense to increase the number of stores, for example, because that's likely to increase total sales. But that doesn't mean sales per store will go up as well. When the cost of opening those stores, supplying them, and staffing them is included, the decision may not increase profitability at all. Faith works the same way: some of what brings momentary profit in this world—competitiveness, one-upsmanship, jockeying for favor—will do little to advance our case in the next.

In Acts 5, after they've been threatened with death, flogged, ordered not to evangelize, and then released, the apostles rejoice. Seems like an odd reaction, right? But we are told it was because "they had been found worthy to suffer dishonor for the sake of the name" (Acts 5:41). In the same way, we find joy when we are able to withstand the temptation of earthly profit, knowing it can never exceed the hope of eternal life we all received in the resurrection.

LOSS

Just as beauty comes with profit, so can everyday life dull its shine. As exciting as that new job seemed on the first day, eventually we stop worrying so much about getting to work on time or finishing that project by the deadline. As dedicated as we were to parenting our infants in the best way possible, by the time they become teenagers, we get tired of fighting about homework and bedtimes and give in. We begin taking advantage of our loved ones in little ways, knowing they'll always be there, so it doesn't matter that much if we allow some space and distance to creep in. We let some space and distance creep into our relationship with God too, because we know he'll always be there. Or will he?

"Therefore, stay awake!" Jesus warns us in Matthew 24:42. "For you do not know on which day your Lord will come." The *Catechism* reminds us that "the chief punishment of hell is eternal separation from God, in whom alone man can possess the life and happiness for which he was created and for which he longs" (CCC, 1035). The more we distance ourselves from God in our earthly lives, the more likely we are to face the ultimate loss, eternal separation.

As Catholics, the sacrament of penance and reconciliation provides us with a visible means of bridging the distance with the Lord, of restoring that which was lost. "In this sacrament, the sinner, placing himself before the merciful judgment of God *anticipates* in a certain way *the judgment* to which he will be subjected at the end of his earthly life. For it is now, in this life, that we are offered the choice between life and death..." (CCC, 1470; emphasis original). Notably, the *Catechism* also reminds us of the need to repair our earthly relationships in the way we interact with others.

Getting stuck in loss, entrenched in our bitterness and fears and self-doubts, keeps us from finding the rest—and profit—the Lord so desires for us. Saying yes to the restoration of peace takes courage and is always rewarded in some way. I think of a friend who went into the confessional trembling and opened with the words, "Bless me, Father, for I have sinned. It's been twenty years since my last confession." And after a pause, the priest responded, "And the angels in heaven are singing at your return." Isn't that a beautiful picture?

A WOMAN OF WORTH

Saint Mary of Egypt

Approximately 344–421 • Feast day – April 1

Mary of Egypt was all about physical profit. She left her parents when she was just twelve, and "unrestrainedly and insatiably gave myself up to sensuality."[4] Sometimes, she accepted payment for this debauchery; other times, not. When she was about thirty, Mary encountered a group of people headed for Jerusalem for the exaltation of the cross and decided to go along, continuing her pattern of random sexual encounters. But something blocked her from entering the temple to see the cross—not once but three or four times. She began praying with an icon of the Blessed Virgin Mary, and she heard her say, "If you cross the Jordan, you will find glorious rest."

Mary drank and bathed in the Jordan River, and in essence became a hermit for nearly fifty years until she encountered a priest named Zosimas and told him her story. When he returned a year later, she was dead.

Mary lost everything she had once valued—her physical attractiveness, her friends and lovers, her fine clothing, her charming personality. Her profit was to know Christ—and to make penance for her sins.

4 http://www.ocf.org/OrthodoxPage/reading/st.mary.html

FINDING YOUR WORTH

1. We always have the potential to bring profit to our relationships: a listening ear, wise counsel, a smile, a story, a hug. We also have the potential to bring loss with our body language, caustic comments, or broken confidences. What profit will you bring today to a challenging relationship?

2. In what ways are you separating yourself from God? Maybe it's something as seemingly simple as not paying attention during a homily or choosing to sleep in rather than begin your day with prayer. How can you rearrange your other priorities to deepen your relationship with God?

3. Are you staying away from the sacrament of penance and reconciliation because you don't believe you can be forgiven? Or, are you continuing to dwell on a matter for which you have been absolved? It's possible that sin is becoming a false idol, crowding out room for God. Talk with a priest about how you might open yourself up to the Lord's mercy with confidence and faith.

Lord, help me to put you first—today and every day—and to deny myself the things that threaten to separate me from you.

CHAPTER 3

OF VOCATION *and* INDUSTRY

She seeks out wool and flax and weaves with skillful hands.

Proverbs 31:13

A recently published Pew Research Center study[5] found that fifty-two percent of Catholics are married; eight percent are living with a partner; seven percent are widowed; and twenty-one percent have never been married. Just twelve percent are divorced or separated.

I'll be honest. As a member of that twelve percent (and, add in the fact that I'm older and childless to the "other"-ness), at times, I feel a little less than valued…and not by the church proper. More than one acquaintance has insisted to me that being a mother and wife is the highest of all ways women can serve the Lord; the religious life is a sort of "runner-up" position; and the rest of us are pitiable also-rans.

Now, we know the woman of worth in Proverbs is married and has children. She loves them. She serves them. But she honors the Lord in other ways

5 http://www.pewresearch.org/fact-tank/2018/03/19/share-of-married-adults-varies-widely-across-u-s-religious-groups/

too. Her vocation is multifaceted, and her service is done with skill and care. In this verse, we look at her weaving.

VOCATION

When you hear the word "vocation," you may think of those called to the priesthood or vowed religious life. But marriage is also a vocation. So is singlehood. Two of our more recent popes addressed vocations in broad, challenging ways.

St. John Paul II in 2001 on the World Day of Prayer for Vocations called vocation "a very good definition of the relationship that God has with every human being in the freedom of love...Vocation is the word that leads us to understand the dynamisms of God's revelation, and thus reveals to man the truth about his existence."[6]

"In God's plan, every man is born to seek self-fulfillment, for every life is called to some task by God," St. Paul VI wrote in *Populorum Progressio*.[7] "At birth a human being possesses certain aptitudes and abilities in germinal form, and these qualities are to be cultivated so that they may bear fruit."

Ah, but it can be confusing as time passes to know that we're doing what we should with those aptitudes and abilities. An acquaintance homeschooled a dozen children. Her large home in the woods is immaculately kept and so inviting to visitors, with flowers, homemade quilts, antique lanterns, and the like. I'm in awe of what she's accomplished. And yet she feels "less than" today. She didn't go to college. She doesn't work outside the home. She doesn't feel she can keep up with others when it comes to spiritual conversations.

A younger friend had had what many people in their twenties consider a dream life: all the right college internships that led to a Capitol Hill job

6 https://w2.vatican.va/content/john-paul-ii/en/messages/vocations/documents/hf_jp-ii_mes_20001125_xxxviii-voc-2001.html

7 http://w2.vatican.va/content/paul-vi/en/encyclicals/documents/hf_p-vi_enc_26031967_populorum.html

with high visibility and even higher stress levels. She then went to work for a major professional organization. Things took a bit of a turn; she married, moved forty miles away from the nation's political epicenter, and had a child. The organization wanted her to stay on, and so she has, part time, working from home. She loves being a wife and mom. But there are still times she feels "less than," spending her days in sweats and leggings instead of power suits.

Here's the thing, sisters. The success or failure of our vocation isn't measured by others' judgment of how important we are. We leave that to the Lord. Our role is to listen and to obey, despite the demons who tell us what we do doesn't matter…or that what we do matters more than what the person next to us is doing. As Paul tells us in Romans 12:4–5: "For as in one body we have many parts, and all the parts do not have the same function, so we, though many, are one body in Christ and individually parts of one another."

INDUSTRY

The Proverbs woman of worth is no slacker. She seeks out the right wool and flax for her work; she doesn't settle. And her weaving is more than a way to pass the time. We know that, because she is described as being skillful at it.

In the same way, carrying out our vocation is not to be done haphazardly. We don't just go through the motions or waste time; we take seriously what the Lord has placed us here to do.

While our vocations may not change, the forms in which we are called to carry them out often do. Changes can throw us for a loop, causing us to freeze in place, afraid of the future or longing for the past rather than continue in an industrious, diligent, conscientious manner.

We find examples throughout the Bible of people who, when they received a call, were industrious with their "yes." Consider the response of Mary when Gabriel shares the news that she will bear the Son of God.

Consider the response of Joseph, who had been planning to quietly divorce Mary when an angel appears to him in a dream. He gets up and immediately takes her into his home. Consider the response of the young John, who, when his dying friend presents Mary as John's mother, immediately takes her into his home.

An acquaintance had two sons and was raising a nephew when her husband died. After five years of discernment, she became a secular Franciscan. A dozen or so years later, she became the foundress of the Family of Jacopa Association, a contemplative/active Franciscan community of women forty and older, both lay and consecrated. Mother Rose Catherine of the Triumph of the Cross, as she's known today, moves ahead with confidence and faith in this vocation, even on the days that her car doesn't start and the community is struggling to pay the utility bills. There's just not time to wring her hands and dwell on things that might or might not happen. Like the Proverbs woman of worth, she looks for the raw material in herself and in those discerning whether to join the community, and she helps God make that raw material into something better.

A WOMAN OF WORTH

Saint Gianna Beretta Molla

1922–1962 • Feast day – April 28

Gianna had just turned twenty when she began medical school. It had been a challenging year; her mother had died a few months earlier. In addition to her studies, Gianna was involved in a variety of church-related charities and organizations. During this period, she wrote: "In one way or another, everyone in society works in the service of humanity."[8] She was twenty-seven when she graduated from medical school; poor health ended her dream of joining her brother, a priest, in Brazil to minister to poor women there. So instead, she opened a clinic.

The week before she turned thirty-three, Gianna married Pietro Molla. She added mother to her vocation soon thereafter, with three children in two and a half years. There was heartbreak as well; Gianna and Pietro also had two miscarriages. It was in the second month of her final pregnancy that Gianna learned she had a uterine tumor. Calling on her faith, she opted to have the tumor removed rather than two other options that would have resulted in the baby's death. After a difficult labor, the baby was born healthy; a week later, Gianna died of an infection that likely would not have been fatal today.

Daughter...sister...doctor...wife...mother...volunteer. Gianna's roles were myriad. (It was a life that also included relaxation, skiing and mountain climbing in particular, and a fondness for fashion.) Vocation was something she gave great thought to, once writing: "What is a vocation? It is a gift from God and therefore comes from God. If then it is a gift from God, it is up to us to do all in our power to know God's will."[9]

8 http://saintgianna.org/medischool.htm

9 http://saintgianna.org/vocsearsh.htm

FINDING YOUR WORTH

1. The saying goes that no one is good at everything, but everyone is good at something. What is it that you're good at? Being a mother, physical or spiritual? Painting? Singing? Listening? Make a list. Ask a friend to help if you can't think of anything.

2. From that list, identify the items that bring you joy. Some of us are good at math or organization, for example, but using those skills saps us mentally, emotionally, and spiritually. Cross out the items in the category. You're likely to find that what remains illumines God's desires for you.

3. The woman of worth chose her tools—wool and flax—with care, and focused on the work at hand, using her skill to craft a pleasing product. What are the tools of your vocation? Are you utilizing them fully, or powering through the task at hand as quickly as possible?

**Lord, I trust in your plans for me.
May I submit with an open and loving heart
to them, even when another path
seems more appealing to me.**

CHAPTER 4

OF SECURING *and* SERVING

Like a merchant fleet, she secures her provisions from afar.

Proverbs 31:14

"Deeds, not words" is the motto of U.S. Merchant Marine Academy graduates. You may not know much about the Merchant Marine, or mariners as they like to be called, and in some ways, that's a good thing.

While the academy on New York's Long Island is a federal service academy, the U.S. Merchant Marine itself consists of commercial ships, owned by private U.S. companies. The mariners are civilians during peacetime, transporting passengers and goods, but officers can be designated as U.S. Navy military officers as needed during times of war or national emergency. The mariners are part of our safety net—not something we think a lot about, but they're a resource that can be called upon in need.

In the same way, women of worth are always ready for service. Wherever we go to do business—the farmers market, the local coffee shop, or on a big girlfriends or family cruise, we bring Christ in ways that aren't always noticeable. We are missionaries with both our deeds and our words, sharing the great bargain that is Christ.

This is how John Gill, an eighteenth-century century Baptist pastor and scholar, looked at this verse:

> She is like the merchant ships ... not like a single one, but like a navy of them ... so the church of Christ, and her true members, like ships of burden, trade to heaven, by prayer and other religious exercises, and return with the riches of grace and mercy, to help them in time of need ... [10]

For purposes of this study, let's consider where and how we as women of worth secure our provisions and then, where and how we deliver them in service.

SECURING

The world's merchant fleet today totals more than 52,000 vessels, according to Statista, a provider of market and consumer data;[11] about 17,000 are general cargo ships. Consider the amount of coordination and prioritization it takes to get those vessels loaded and from Point A to Point B and on time amid the vagaries of manufacturing, weather, and so on. If a shipment arrives too early, time and money can be wasted in port until the next conveyance model is ready to move the goods on. If a shipment arrives too late, the merchant's opportunity may be lost. Selecting the right route for your budget and desired arrival date is critical; for example, a vessel traveling at a speed of ten knots from Baltimore has five options for its journey to the Indian port of Mumbai, ranging in time from thirty-five to seventy-six days.[12]

10 http://biblehub.com/commentaries/gill/proverbs/31.htm

11 https://www.statista.com/statistics/264024/number-of-merchant-ships-worldwide-by-type/

12 https://sea-distances.org/

In the woman of worth's day, piracy also would have been an issue, and while it's not as prevalent today, it still happens. Remember about ten years ago when pirates were wreaking havoc in the waters off Somalia? One Earth Future's Oceans Beyond Piracy program reported that the Horn of Africa, West Africa, and Southeast Asia remain areas of concern.[13]

Our faith lives are a lot like merchant fleets. We know where we are today, and we know where we want to complete our trip—in the Lord's loving arms in the place he has prepared for us. But there are plenty of obstacles to getting there: our own inertia, lack of knowledge, pride, ignorance, fear, and so on. It's easy to get blown off course or to be the victims of the devil's piracy of our souls. It's also tempting at times to leave our God-directed "shipping lanes" and look for shortcuts and tantalizing detours.

How do we remain securely on course? With the Lord, of course, the best safety net ever. Consider some of the awesome protections he offers us.

Why did the woman of worth seek provisions from afar? Because she was particular about the materials she used. Perhaps they weren't available locally or the local goods were of inferior quality. She wanted only the best for her household and was willing to invest the time and effort to ensure that. Consider the way you are providing for your own or your family's spiritual well-being. Do you slide out of Mass after the Eucharist so that you can get the kids to soccer or lacrosse matches? Do you skimp on church financial contributions so that you can have the latest mobile phone and the finest home furnishings? Do you figure you'll get around to praying someday...someday when your life is less chaotic? Do you look for the best price, without considering the quality of the product or the sacrificed dignity of the workers who made it? We grieve the Lord and, yes, reject his outstretched hands when we make stuff more important than he and his people. We undermine our own security, and leave our souls open to the devil's piracy.

13 http://oceansbeyondpiracy.org/publications/state-maritime-piracy-2017

SERVING

Yes, the woman of worth was careful about where she acquired her provisions. In doing so, she showed the others in her household, family and servants, that they mattered to her. Her care likely included ensuring that the food they ate was prepared properly, that the furniture was sturdy and well made, and that the furnishings were tasteful and pleasing to the eye. For her, it wasn't just about having "stuff" for herself; she also served others in her choices. Today, we'd call her a servant leader, someone whose life purpose is to help others achieve their dreams and goals, and to provide a safe place for their pursuit.

You might say Jesus was among the original servant leaders. He tells us in Mark 10:42–44:

> "You know that those who are recognized as rulers over the Gentiles lord it over them, and their great ones make their authority over them felt. But it shall not be so among you. Rather, whoever wishes to become great among you will be your servant; whoever wishes to be first among you will be the slave of all."

Jesus does more than talk about servant leadership. He shows it to us at the Last Supper as he bends down to wash and dry the disciples' feet. After gently setting aside Peter's protestation and completing the washing, he tells them, "I have given you a model to follow, so that as I have done for you, you should also do" (John 13:15).

Jesus could have easily instructed the disciples to wash each other's feet, or to wash his. But that wouldn't have shown them the way he desired them to serve.

Think about it. Do we as women of worth follow his example? Do we serve with humility and love, putting the best of ourselves forward, or do we hold back the best wine? Do we take the same care with our appearance when we volunteer at a food pantry as when we are going to Mass?

Do we spend as much time selecting the right ingredients for a parish event casserole as when we're planning our own Thanksgiving dinner? Do we greet the stranger who asks us for directions or spare change with the same warmth as when we have an unexpected encounter with a friend?

I worked for a while in a fairly toxic environment. There'd been a merger, and those of us on staff were trying to puzzle out whether there was a place for us in the new structure. Many of those in leadership were focused on securing their own place, not on our trepidations. One executive stood out. Anytime I saw him encounter someone at headquarters or in his field office seven hundred miles away, his face lit up as if he'd just seen a long-lost friend, and out went his hand. I don't think he knew everyone's name, but it didn't matter. During a stressful time, he seemed to take true delight in every encounter. His style has helped to smooth emotions and tempers among those who remain with the organization and to begin to rebuild trust.

Serving with a grimace or rolled eyes isn't service. Serving our cheap, less than palatable wine or castoff, second-rate provisions to anyone—family, friends, or strangers—isn't service. It's ego and convenience and expediency. Service is offering up all of ourselves to show others the way to salvation, just as Jesus did on the cross.

A WOMAN OF WORTH

Saint Frances Cabrini

1850–1917 • Feast day – November 13

Frances Cabrini was a frail child but dreamed of a life of service even then; one story has it that she would send "missionary" flowers in little paper boats down a stream. Because of her health, she was unsuccessful in finding a community of women religious who would accept her. Ultimately, she and others founded the Missionary Sisters of the Sacred Heart of Jesus. When Frances met with Pope Leo XIII to gain permission for missionary service in China, he counseled her to go to the United States instead, because it was teeming with Italian emigrants.

From the time she and six other sisters arrived in New York City in 1889 until her death thirty years later, Frances cajoled, nagged, and prayed to get donations of time, talent, and treasure for the sixty-seven hospitals, schools, and orphanages she founded on three continents. She wasn't shy about it, counseling, "Search among your acquaintances, among those who feel the desire to do something good for God's glory, good souls who want to become coworkers."[14] She expected people to give their best, not just what they had left over after their own wants and desires were taken care of.

On December 22, 1917, Frances was not well. Still, she spent part of the day wrapping candy for children's Christmas gifts. It was a task she could have easily delegated to others and instead taken to her bed. Frances died later that day, having given both God and those in need her best, even at the last.

14 https://www.mothercabrini.org/who-we-are/cabrinian-laity/

FINDING YOUR WORTH

1. Identify an area where the pirate is trying to take you off course. Maybe it's whispers that you have too much else to do to pray or that it really doesn't matter if you're unkind to a family member or friend, because he or she will always love you. Think about what you can do to set things right. Consult a priest or other spiritual adviser as needed.

2. Where are you mailing in your ministry rather than serving—in your home, your neighborhood, your parish, or in some activity? How can you rearrange your priorities, including saying a compassionate no to some activities, so that you become a servant in the manner of Jesus?

3. Frances Cabrini believed that good souls "want to become coworkers." Invite someone to join you in a service activity. (A home activity, such as cleaning or cooking, qualifies!) If that person says no, look for another "good soul."

Jesus, help me to serve as you served on earth, humbly and confidently, with eyes always on the Father.

CHAPTER 5

OF RISING *and* PROVIDING

She rises while it is still night, and distributes food to her household, a portion to her maidservants.
Proverbs 31:15

Each December, I attempt to complete a beautiful Filipino tradition, the Simbang Gabi ("Night Mass") novena. There's lots of praying, singing, and sharing of Spirit-filled food and conversation. It's the rare day we don't get at least one hundred fifty people at a nearby parish, and on weekends the number is more like five hundred. There's just one thing: Mass starts at 5 AM. That's right, nine days of Mass at 5 AM, amid the busyness and physical darkness of Advent. When the tradition began centuries ago in the Philippines, the idea was that fishers and farmers would start their day with the Masses, preparing them for work and disrupting schedules less than if the Masses were offered after work.

As for Simbang Gabi here, even for those like me who live a few blocks away, the novena means rising at 4:15 or 4:30 AM. It's still dark when we all go our own ways around 6:45 or 7 after we've celebrated and had breakfast together. It's not unusual for the celebrant to say "good evening" rather than "good morning" in welcoming the congregation.

And none of that matters to any of us. We're there to prepare ourselves for Jesus's coming, to accept with humility the endless gifts he provides us, and to support each other where we can with tangible and intangible food for the journey.

RISING

Rising, regardless of the hour, can be difficult. More than physical tiredness can tempt us to hit the snooze button or dismiss the alarm altogether. A Centers for Disease Control and Prevention study[15] found that more than a third of American adults don't get enough sleep on a regular basis (seven or more hours daily). We've all heard—and probably ignored—the tips for remedying this: going to bed and rising at the same time each day, turning off electronics, and so on.

But sometimes, we just don't want to face the challenges in our families, our jobs, our caregiving, and elsewhere. Every day can begin to feel the same in a soul-numbing way—get up, get ready, feel less than adequate, go to bed, repeat. Even if we rise physically, our souls sleepwalk through the hours. We might call it apathy or numbness. But whatever we name it, we know that today will be just like yesterday, and tomorrow will be just like today. The situation is beyond our control, so why not spend another fifteen minutes or an hour in bed? It's not like anything will change if we do.

The woman of worth, however, has hope in the day and faith in the Lord, even if yesterday wasn't so great. She rises to do his work. And with Christ's help, we can do the same. In 2018's *Gaudete et Exsultate,* Pope Francis encouraged that our missions on earth be considered paths of holiness, noting: "That mission has its fullest meaning in Christ, and can only be understood through him. At its core, holiness is experiencing, in union with Christ, the mysteries of his life. It consists in uniting ourselves

15 https://www.cdc.gov/media/releases/2016/p0215-enough-sleep.html

to the Lord's death and resurrection in a unique and personal way, constantly dying and rising anew with him."[16]

We see examples of people in states of great distress doing the same in Scripture. We are told in John 20:1 that "on the first day of the week, Mary of Magdala came to the tomb early in the morning, while it was still dark . . ." Just two days earlier, she had seen her friend and teacher stripped, beaten, and crucified. She was grieving. Perhaps she also had some concerns for her own safety. But she had to get up early to prepare Jesus for burial. It was her duty and obligation. Fulfilling that responsibility, John tells us, gave her the honor of being the first of the followers to see the risen Christ.

Indeed, Jesus showed examples of rising throughout his earthly ministry. In Matthew 9:6, he tells the paralytic to rise and pick up his stretcher. In Luke 7:14, the widow's son at Nain is returned from the dead with the words, "Young man, I tell you, rise!" In Mark 5:41, he commands the synagogue leader's dead daughter to get up. In his own agony in the garden, after praying that the cup might be removed, he returned to his sleeping disciples and girded himself for what was to come, confident in the Father's promise of the ultimate rising—the resurrection.

PROVIDING

At the very start of her day, the woman of worth makes certain that all the members of her household, including the servants, will be fed. That's her top priority; everything else will be dealt with as the hours pass. There's a beautiful rhythm and respect to her routine.

Making sure that others are cared for—physically, emotionally, and spiritually—is something at which we as women excel. That's true in our traditional roles as wives, mothers, nurses, teachers, and servers, but it's also the case in the board room and on the construction site. Here's how St. John Paul II put it in his 1995 letter to women:

16 http://w2.vatican.va/content/francesco/en/apost_exhortations/documents/papa-francesco_esortazione-ap_20180319_gaudete-et-exsultate.html#_ftn47

> For in giving themselves to others each day, women fulfill their deepest vocation. Perhaps more than men, women *acknowledge the person*, because they see persons with their hearts. They see them independently of various ideological or political systems. They see others in their greatness and limitations; they try to go out to them and *help them*.[17] (emphasis original)

How do we help? Surely, by preparing meals for those who depend upon us as well as ourselves. But there's something deeper than bag lunches and sandwiches here. Food that fills a grocery cart or a hungry person's stomach is important. So is the food that feeds hearts and souls in the way we interact with others. It can be as simple as hugging children when we send them off to school, asking about a colleague's sick mother, or listening patiently to a friend's story we've already heard several times. It can be a smile for the homeless man you see every week on your way to Mass. It can be asking the name of the woman who comes to the food pantry each week while you're volunteering.

And the earlier in our day that we start, regardless of the hour we rise, the more we can serve.

17 https://w2.vatican.va/content/john-paul-ii/en/letters/1995/documents/hf_jp-ii_let_29061995_women.html

A WOMAN OF WORTH

Saint Jeanne Delanoue

1666–1736 • Feast day – August 17

Jeanne Delanoue was all about business. By the time she was twenty-four, Jeanne was running the family's shop that sold religious articles near a popular pilgrimage site in France's Loire Valley. She also rented out rooms to pilgrims. The shop operated even on Sundays and holy days, despite the disapproval of local Catholics. (That practice changed when the priest whom Jeanne wanted as a spiritual adviser refused to help her unless she closed on those days.)

Still, the change in operating hours did not affect the shop owner's heart. One biographer wrote that "Jeanne's piety was of the scrupulous kind. She was very anxious to be truthful, so she told the poor people she had 'no bread in the house;' and she calculated exactly what was needed for each meal, bought it at the time, and had not a scrap over."[18]

In 1693, Jeanne tried to send away Françoise Souchet, a pilgrim she knew had scarce financial means. Undeterred, Françoise spoke of poverty and thanksgiving. After a mystical experience, Jeanne began working with the poor and eventually closed the shop. She spent the rest of her life assisting orphans, young girls, elderly, and poor through the community she founded, St. Anne of Providence of Saumur. It is said that Jeanne frequently arose at 3 AM to wander the streets in search of people who needed help. Her conversion story challenges us to rise and do the Lord's work as well.

18 Taylor, Frances Margaret. *A Marvellous History, or the Life of Jeanne de la Noue* (Burns and Oates: London, 1884), p. 4.

FINDING YOUR WORTH

1. Is an alarm going off in your faith life—but you keep hitting snooze? Think about how you might answer it. See if shifting your prayer time to a different part of the day will serve you better.

2. What sort of service example are you setting for your family and others? Do you demand effusive thanks for all the tasks you do for them? Just for today, perform those tasks as a form of sacrifice and thanks for the Lord's goodness, expecting nothing from those you serve.

3. Where in your ministry are you going through the motions rather than truly acknowledging the person? Make a list of three situations you will try to change. Small changes are fine!

Lord, I ask for clarity in knowing what you desire of me, so that I may rise in faith and confidence to do your will.

CHAPTER 6

OF FORESIGHT *and* PRODUCTION

She picks out a field and acquires it; from her earnings she plants a vineyard.

Proverbs 31:16

There's a saying among those who know and make wine: "The worse the soil, the better the wine." What we generally consider to be good soil—not too much clay, not too much sand, not too much alkaline or acidity, not too much anything—tends to result in too much vine and too little flavor. If the soil is that good, expert pruning is needed.

Winemaking isn't for the impatient or the easily discouraged. It can be three years before a new vineyard yields its first harvest. After the grapes are picked and sorted, there's still more to be done: crushing and pressing, fermentation, clarification, aging, and bottling. If you're making wine for yourself, you can have something to drink after a month or so, though you'd probably be happier with the result if you waited a year or, depending on the composition, even longer.

Tended properly, a vineyard can produce for more than a hundred years. It's something that can be passed from generation to generation.

What kind of vineyard is your faith? The Bible is rich in analogies about vines. Let's look at a few.

FORESIGHT

The woman of worth didn't buy just any field. She assessed her resources and her plans and the properties available. And when the right one presented itself, she was ready to move. Maybe it was a piece of land others bypassed because of the soil quality, the location, the slope, or the amount of work that would be required to make it arable. But the woman of worth recognized its value. Her wisdom brings to mind the parable Jesus told in Matthew 13:44: "The kingdom of heaven is like a treasure buried in a field, which a person finds and hides again, and out of joy goes and sells all that he has and buys that field."

Sometimes, we overvalue our own "fields." We know intellectually that the Lord is supposed to come first, but how will our son get a coveted college lacrosse scholarship if he's not on the high school traveling team—and that means games on Saturdays and Sundays? How will we get that big promotion and the big money it will bring if we're not on call 24/7 for a critical project? How will we manage to pay for the home remodel if we don't cut back on our tithing? We tell ourselves that God will understand. Oh yes, he will understand. And he will grieve. Because when the best treasure is found and in front of us, why would we think looking elsewhere is more important?

Do we "acquire" God, or does God acquire us? Maybe a little of both, at the outset. We take each other on with our baptism, and we confirm the ongoing acquisition throughout sacraments. Eventually, we come to understand that the Lord offers himself to us freely, and in exchange asks only for love. That love, however, involves more than going to Mass and praying. It means living a life of obedience and surrender, giving up more and more of ourselves as we attempt to reach the depths of that love.

God showed his ultimate love in the sacrifice of his Son and his resurrection. We wonder sometimes about whether we are worth the price of that acquisition. We may not think so, but he surely does. Remember

Jeremiah 1:5? "Before I formed you in the womb I knew you, before you were born I dedicated you, a prophet to the nations I appointed you." He picked us out, just as carefully as the woman of worth selected her field!

PRODUCTION

The woman of worth didn't expect her vineyard to turn a profit immediately. She was patient, planting it, watering it, pruning it, and loving it before the vines produced usable grapes. In the same way, the Lord believes that, with patience, we will produce fruit.

In John 15, Jesus describes himself as "the true vine"; the Father as the vine grower, and all of us as the branches. He speaks of the Lord's vigilant pruning, removing every branch that bears no fruit. Jesus goes on to say: "Whoever remains in me and I in him will bear much fruit, because without me you can do nothing" (John 15:5).

And fruitful, we are called to be. The Lord is not particularly gentle with vineyards that are willful in their lack of production: "What more could be done for my vineyard that I did not do?... Now, I will let you know what I am going to do with my vineyard: Take away its hedge, give it to grazing, break through its wall, let it be trampled!" (Isaiah 5:4–5).

Just how much a vineyard produces in any given year varies, despite the grower's best efforts. While there's some control to be had over watering and pruning, growers have little they can do about the number of sunny versus cloudy days. Pesticides can help with mites, beetles, spiders, and other vermin, but new, hardier enemies crop up. Think about our vineyards, and the evil one's constant efforts to worm his way into our souls. Without the Father's love and care and patience, our production would be nil.

Talk of grapevines and their fruit always brings to mind my favorite of Jesus's stories: the parable of the workers. You know the story: at the end of the day, the landowner makes the *exact same payment* to the workers who started early in the morning, at mid-morning, at midday, at mid-afternoon, and in late afternoon. Not surprisingly, the early-morning folks grumble, even though they received the pay they had been promised. The owner replies: "Am I not free to do as I wish with my own money? Are you envious because I am generous?" (Matthew 20:15). I love this story for obvious reasons, as someone who was away from faith for decades. More importantly, it shows the Lord's great enduring desire for us to be part of his vineyard.

"God is patient with us because he loves us, and those who love are able to understand, to hope, to inspire confidence," Pope Francis said in an April 2013 homily. "God always waits for us, even when we have left him behind! He is never far from us, and if we return to him, he is ready to embrace us."[19]

A WOMAN OF WORTH

Saint Maria Goretti

1890–1902 • Feast day – July 6

Maria Goretti knew a lot about fields and crops. They were all that stood between her family and utter destitution, and the safety zone grew smaller and smaller as time went on.

Her parents lost the family farm by the time Maria was five, and they were forced to work the fields of others to survive. When she was nine, her father died, leaving her mother and siblings to do field work while Maria took care of the housework and the baby. Circumstances were such that they shared a house with a father and son, Giovanni and Alessandro Serenelli. Twenty-year-old Alessandro, however, was more focused on having his way with Maria than in work. Frustrated by her refusal, he stabbed her with a metal file fourteen times.

19 http://w2.vatican.va/content/francesco/en/homilies/2013/documents/papa-francesco_20130407_omelia-possesso-cattedra-laterano.html

Maria died the following day. But before that, somehow, the child saw what God saw in her murderer. She identified Alessandro, forgave him, and said she would see him in heaven.

It took years for Alessandro's conversion to come to fruition, sparked by Maria's appearance to him offering fourteen white lilies, one for each of her wounds. In 1934, five years after his release from prison, he went to Maria's mother and pleaded with her for forgiveness. His act had not only taken her daughter but had resulted in the breakup of her family due to the resulting financial straits. Maria's mother replied she had to forgive him, as her daughter had.

Reports differ as to whether Alessandro, who spent his post-release life as a Capuchin convent gardener and caretaker, was physically present when Maria was canonized in 1950. That doesn't really matter; what does is that her faith and the Lord managed to cultivate a garden in a plot that was once suitable only for weeds.

FINDING YOUR WORTH

1. The Lord is calling you to take a chance on him. Where are you hedging your bets instead of saying yes to his plans for you?

2. What needs to be pruned back in your life so that your faith can become more of a priority?

3. Offer a Rosary or other prayer for someone who has grievously injured you. Pray that his or her eyes will be opened to the Lord's love.

Master Gardener, may I be open to your pruning so that I might produce the fruit you desire.

CHAPTER 7

OF STRENGTH *and* VIGOR

She girds herself with strength; she exerts her arms with vigor.

Proverbs 31:17

We get our strength from a lot of places: Time at the gym or in our favorite non-couch-potato sport. Running, jogging, or walking marathons. Hiking. Mountain climbing. Biking. Swimming. Chasing after the kids or grandkids. Physical activity can help to ward off all sorts of ailments, and it benefits us mentally, spiritually, and emotionally too. We are blessed to live in an age when muscles on a woman are not considered unladylike.

Our faith benefits from a good workout as well. When we simply go through the motions at Mass or limit our prayer lives to a litany of complaints, questions, and directives just before we nod off to sleep, we become flabby. We miss out on the benefits offered by studying Scripture, sacred Tradition, and written works. We miss out on the growth we can experience by engaging in new ministries and taking our beliefs into uncomfortable places. When we exert our arms with vigor as women of worth, we find Jesus waiting to hug us.

STRENGTH

Christianity has never been for sissies. Now, it's not like anyone is preventing us today from attending Mass or reading the Bible or preparing for or receiving the sacraments. But think of all the seemingly small means by which your faith can be challenged. Businesses can be penalized in very real ways if the owners' beliefs run counter to the law. Our friends and colleagues assume everyone holds the same worldview as they do on hot-button issues such as abortion, same-gender marriage, euthanasia, capital punishment, and immigration, and look at us pityingly when they find we don't. Even outward signs such as our foreheads on Ash Wednesday and our abstinence from meat on Lenten Fridays become topics for "teasing."

Indeed, people who are uneducated about Christianity or who choose to ridicule it are problems. But so are we when we don't respond to attacks with love and with knowledge. Every challenge is an opportunity for evangelization and an opportunity to build our own strength. St. Paul's conversion may have culminated on the road to Damascus, but it didn't start there. It started when St. Stephen spoke truth to those who called it blasphemy and were preparing to stone him.

The evil that led to St. Stephen's martyrdom (and St. Paul's, for that matter) still exists. Evil likes crowds; groupthink makes it difficult for us to stand up for the Lord. We find it's easier to be quiet or, perhaps even worse, go along to get along. Evil likes those quiet times and the opportunities to tell us that our weaknesses are shameful—or that we gain strength by persecuting others or by isolating ourselves from anyone who is different from us. Those insidious little whispers wear down our fortitude and darken our minds and souls.

Amid these internal and external attacks, where do we find our spiritual strength? In the Lord, of course. St. Paul exhorts us to "draw your strength from the Lord and from his mighty power" (Ephesians 6:10), and in Ephesians 6:13–17 provides an impressive list of the weapons we are given:

- The armor of God
- Righteousness as a breastplate
- Shoes ready for the gospel of peace
- The shield of faith
- The helmet of salvation
- The sword of the Spirit

Others may not see our spiritual armor. But we know it is there. We acquire it by removing ourselves from temptations, by prayer, by study, by activity, by finding solace and support in our communities, whether that be our families, our convents and monasteries, our parishes, or other refuges. And when we strap it on, we will always be victorious over evil and those who seek to destroy us and him, even when the bullets and rocks and knives maim or kill our bodies, because those wounds bring us closer in the body of Christ.

"I have the strength for everything through him who empowers me," St. Paul tells the Philippians (Philippians 4:13). He doesn't say, "I shall emerge victorious in this world and wipe out all my enemies." He doesn't say, "Even if they win this time, I'll be ready for payback time when it comes." He doesn't say, "I'm scared. Let someone stronger do the job." Paul's words give us a path ahead, help us to be ready for whatever the world throws at us.

OF VIGOR

Think of vigor as robustness, of strength in activity. It was an attribute much commented upon in the Old Testament. (Interestingly, the word appears but once in this edition of the New Testament, when a man named Apollos argues the Scriptures show that Jesus is the Messiah.) It's noted that when Moses died at one hundred and twenty years old: "his eyes were undimmed and his vigor unabated" (Deuteronomy 34:7).

When Judas Maccabee presses his first division "with the utmost vigor" (2 Maccabees 12:23) against the enemy, as many as 30,000 are destroyed.

Vigor results when we treat our bodies the way the Lord desires. Our vigor is sapped when we become couch potatoes, when we overindulge in food, alcohol, narcotics, and other substances and practices. Paul reminds us that our bodies are "a temple of the Holy Spirit" and do not belong to us: "For you have been purchased at a price. Therefore glorify God in your body" (1 Corinthians 6:20). If we fail to do that, our spiritual vigor dissipates.

Our faith is one lived in community. For most of us, that's our parish. "The parish is where the Church lives," the U.S. Conference of Catholic Bishops wrote recently in introducing its "Communities of Salt and Light" endeavor aimed at strengthening local social ministries. "Parishes are the place where God's people meet Jesus in word and sacrament and come in touch with the source of the Church's life."[20] Our parish is critical to building our strength and offering our vigor. If we believe it does neither, then maybe that's the first place for us to consider rolling up our sleeves and pitching in.

Is it a surprise that the vigor of the woman of worth's arms are called out in Proverbs? I don't think so. There is a physical robustness to the practice of our faith. We see it at Mass when we strike our breasts to confess our faults, kneel during the consecration, encounter each other during the sign of peace, and come forward to receive the Eucharist. Vigor is also a requirement in the way we do service: holding a child, carrying groceries for a food pantry customer, shoveling snow for a neighbor, hugging a grieving friend. When we are active, we bring Christ's strength to those who need it most. When we choose not to help, to let our arms fall at our sides or fold them across our chests, we atrophy, physically and spiritually.

20 http://www.usccb.org/beliefs-and-teachings/what-we-believe/catholic-social-teaching/communities-of-salt-and-light-reflections-on-the-social-mission-of-the-parish.cfm

A WOMAN OF WORTH

Saint Bernadette Soubirous

1844–1879 • Feast day – April 16

Physically, there wasn't much strength or vigor to Bernadette Soubirous. She suffered from cholera as a toddler and was severely asthmatic, a condition that surely was not helped by living with her parents and siblings in a damp, cramped, one-room home that had once served as a jail cell. Chronic ill health kept her from becoming a Carmelite nun; instead, she joined a Sisters of Charity community, where she spent a good share of her time as a patient in the infirmary. When asked by another sister why she remained in bed, she said: I am doing my job: to be ill."[21] Tuberculosis would claim her within a few months of her thirty-third birthday.

But her spiritual strength was as impressive as her earthly strength was not. Bernadette was unmoved by hours and days of questioning by civil and clerical officials about the eighteen times the Blessed Virgin appeared to her in a six-month period. When the officials altered her testimony, she corrected it. When her mental stability was questioned and other children shunned her, she ignored the slights. Bernadette took no personal credit for her strength or for being the one selected to see the Blessed Virgin. "I was nothing, and of this nothing God made something great,"[22] she would write later.

Bernadette's life shows us that spiritual strength is available to all if we exercise it and fortify it with prayer and time with the Lord.

21 Roy, François. "The Personality of Saint Bernadette," *The Furrow* (September 1958), p. 588.

22 http://www.ewtn.com/library/mary/bernlife.htm

FINDING YOUR WORTH

1. Review the list of spiritual weapons from Ephesians 6. Which do you most need to take into battle in a challenging relationship? How can you use that weapon to prepare to interact with compassionate strength in your next encounter with the person?

2. Before the next time you go to Mass, write down the number of times your posture will change. Rather than just going through the motions, think about why we stand, sit, and kneel when we do. Talk about it with a family member or friend afterward.

3. Engage in some physical activity for the Lord this week. Some ways you might do this include volunteering at the parish nursery, doing yardwork for a neighbor, or serving as a greeter at Mass, a homeless shelter, or food pantry.

Lord, strengthen my arms, my legs, my mind, and my soul, so that I might serve you with robustness and vigor.

CHAPTER 8

OF DEALINGS *and* READINESS

She enjoys the profit from her dealings; her lamp is never extinguished at night.

Proverbs 31:18

How in the world does the woman of worth make time for everything described in Proverbs 31? I think the key is in the first part of this verse. She doesn't waste her time on junk. At work, she treats her customers and suppliers fairly so that all may benefit. At home, she treats her family and servants with respect and love. She's present in her interactions; you wouldn't see the woman of worth with her face in her mobile phone at dinner or as she's driving or walking down the sidewalk.

Now all of this does not mean she's never at leisure. She does sleep, of course; her ever-lit lamp is internal, not external. But her free time also shows profit: dinners with friends where the conversation doesn't involve gossip or complaining. Family time that has laughter and honest sharing about problems and joy at celebrations. Vacation time spent feeding her mind, body, and spirit.

The woman of worth shows us that profit isn't always about dollars and cents and figuring out how to get more than the next person. Here, profit is the confidence that what we do is what the Lord desires.

DEALINGS

Some scams are obvious—like the email I received today from the Federal Bureau of Investigation director advising me that $10.3 million is waiting for me in a bank due to the government's past illegal activities, or the phone calls from the Internal Revenue Service warning that "the cops" will come to my home and arrest me if I don't settle up right away.

Others are more difficult to identify, because they pull at our heartstrings. Maybe that woman who came up to you in tears and asked for twenty dollars because she ran out of gas three blocks away and her four sick children are in the car is telling the truth. Of course, if you see her telling the same story tomorrow, maybe not.

Why do people run scams? I'd like to think because they're desperate, or were at some point, and ran into walls getting legitimate work or assistance. Earning a less than ethical living may put food on the table, but it drains the soul and hardens the heart. If we see others as marks and suckers, we diminish them and ourselves.

The woman of worth, conversely, is above board in her dealings, personal and professional. We know she is generous to her family and those in need, monetarily and with her time and skills. She is able to do that in part because of the profit she attains as an honest woman. The woman of worth doesn't work with suppliers who are able to provide the cheapest price because their employees work in sweatshops. She also doesn't mark up her goods outrageously just because she knows the market will bear it.

Our world is full of duplicity. We see it in our political leaders who publicly champion respect for women while disrespecting them in private life; in priests who appeared so effective at pastoral duties but were abusing children; in privately held businesses that give employees a one-hundred-dollar bonus when tax laws are changed, then pocket millions. The woman of worth's world is the same wherever she is; you wouldn't look at the Internet one day and find her private conduct is at odds with her public image. She knows she is ultimately answerable to the Master.

In each of the synoptic gospels, Jesus asks what profit there would be in gaining the world but losing our souls. As women of worth, we know the answer is zero, and conduct ourselves accordingly.

READINESS

You know the parable of the ten virgins: the women go to meet the bridegroom, but he's delayed. When he finally comes, they're called to trim their wicks so that their flames will be bright and clean. But five women's lamps are running out of oil. The other five refuse to share, so the first five have to go buy more, and by the time they get back, everyone's at the wedding feast and they are locked out. When they knock, the Lord says, "Amen, I say to you, I do not know you" (Matthew 25:12).

Pretty harsh on the Lord's part, right? And what about those five "wise" virgins: Couldn't they have shared a little oil, or shined the way for everyone?

Not really, and no.

The parable makes us uncomfortable in the same way Jesus's discourse on discipleship makes us feel uncomfortable: "If anyone comes to me without hating his father and mother, wife and children, brothers and sisters, and even his own life, he cannot be my disciple" (Luke 14:26).

The woman of worth is ready. She loves her life today, and those in it. But her faith is her light, and she will never let it go out, regardless of all the people and dealings and events that are important to her in this world. She nourishes that light through prayer, study, and other resources.

The Lord wants us to be ready for *him, now,* 24/7. Not after we help our friends. Not after we get the kids through school. Not after we retire. *Now.* After all, the greatest commandment is to love God with all our heart, soul, and mind. If something or someone else takes precedence over him in any of those places, we have a problem.

It can be hard for us as women to say no to requests for assistance. After all, we're wives, mothers, daughters, sisters, employees, and volunteers, and you might say it's in our very nature to put ourselves second, third, or even lower as we attempt to keep everyone happy. But the lower the priority we make ourselves, the lower the priority we give God, and the more dangerously low the oil in our lamps becomes.

In his *Lumen Fidei,* Pope Francis drew the same analogy and sounded a warning: "once the flame of faith dies out, all other lights begin to dim. The light of faith is unique, since it is capable of illuminating *every aspect* of human existence" (emphasis original).[23] May we remember that true women of worth understand that—and live it.

23 http://w2.vatican.va/content/francesco/en/encyclicals/documents/papa-francesco_20130629_enciclica-lumen-fidei.html

A WOMAN OF WORTH

Saint Marie-Azélie Guérin Martin

1831–1877 • Feast day – July 12

Zelie, as she was known, kept her lamp lit as she listened to the Lord and adjusted her path. She considered religious life, but was rejected by the Sisters of Charity for health reasons. Zelie then took up lacemaking; her work won awards, and she was regarded as an excellent businesswoman and employer. She met Louis Martin when she was twenty-six, and they were married three months later. Eventually, he would sell his watchmaking business to work with Zelie.

The Martins had nine children, only five of whom lived past the age of five. As we all know, all the daughters became women religious, including the youngest, who would become St. Thérèse of Lisieux. Zelie was just forty-five when she learned she had breast cancer, and she died less than a year later.

Through it all, she appeared calm, according to her daughters and her letters, including this: "Several people said to me, 'It would have been better never to have had [the four children who died young],' but I could not endure this sort of language. I did not think that the sufferings and anxieties could be weighed in the same scale of the eternal happiness of my children. They were not lost forever; life is short and full of miseries, and we shall find them again up yonder."[24] Her example of obedience and readiness can help us all as we seek to draw closer to the Lord.

24 Piat, Stephane and Joseph Piat. *The Story of a Family: The Home Life of the Little Flower* (New York: P.J. Kenedy & Sons, 1948), .p. 98.

FINDING YOUR WORTH

1. Is an occasional "treat" to yourself—chocolate, social media, gossiping—taking up more and more time or soul space? Keep track for one day of the minutes or hours you're using. Is this "treat" crowding out activities that would lead to spiritual profit? Try cutting back or eliminating this treat, just for a week. Journal about your withdrawal feelings.

2. Where are you seeking profit in your dealings in a non-spiritual way? Being less than loving to your children, family, or friends by demanding a relationship exist on your terms? Cutting corners at work (coming in late, leaving early, not meeting due dates)? Letting your mind wander during Mass? What can you do to help these encounters bear fruit?

3. Identify the commitments that are threatening to deplete your lamp oil reserves. Talk with a priest or trusted friend or adviser about how to say a loving no to some of what you do, and yes to more time resting in the Lord. Ask this person to help hold you accountable.

Lord, I feel pulled in so many directions today. I don't want to let people down. Guide my way so that you are first in my priorities, and that I reflect you in the ministry you do through me.

CHAPTER 9

OF HUMILITY *and* GUIDANCE

She puts her hands to the distaff, and her fingers ply the spindle.

Proverbs 31:19

It's a tricky, labor-intensive business, spinning by hand. In preparing to write this chapter, I spent a fair amount of time watching demo videos to understand the process and would encourage you to check out a few to gain an appreciation for the way this was all done before spinning wheels and machines took over.

In one hand, or on something propped near you, is the distaff, a pole or stick about three feet long that's loaded with the flax or wool or whatever raw material you're using. The other hand guides the spindle, about a foot long with a hook or notch on it. The spindle spins, teasing yarn out of the fiber. If the yarn breaks, no worries; take a bit of water and twist together the yarn near its end and a new strand of fiber. The whole process is complicated by knowing how much twist or spin to use.

It says a lot about the woman of worth that she engaged in spinning, rather than leaving it solely for her maids. To me, it shows her humility and her desire to serve as an example to others.

OF HUMILITY

We know from the other verses in Proverbs that this is a wealthy, busy woman. Why does she take the time to sit with her servants to share in this somewhat mind-numbing task? Perhaps she also wants to show her servants that all tasks are important and no chore is beneath her, regardless of her station.

A friend of mine spent decades moving around the globe as a high-ranking American Foreign Service career employee. She was quoted in news articles and represented our government ably. She had the kind of security clearance she's not allowed to talk about. She took early retirement in part to care for her ailing husband and did not spend a night away from him for the seven years leading up to his death. She oversaw home renovations, including installation of an elevator, to make him more comfortable. She advocated for him with innumerable medical professionals. She sat by his side for hours on end in hospitals and hospice. I never heard her say a single word about him being a burden or wanting her old life back. She regarded it as a privilege to take on all these unfamiliar tasks on his behalf. When he died, she was heartbroken.

That sort of humble, quiet service doesn't win awards or draw public attention. But it does inspire those of us who watch it. If we let those examples take root in our souls, we grow in humility ourselves.

Living in humility can be difficult, especially when we know we're not the ones at fault. But we are called to do it in all situations: "Who among you is wise and understanding? Let him show his works by a good life in the humility that comes from wisdom" (James 3:13).

I ended up on parish council less than a month after I returned to Catholicism. (I thought I was volunteering for Sunday doughnuts duty.) That was hard for me and for others, chief among them the pastor, the Rev. Gerry Creedon, who died in 2017. I didn't like a lot about his management style—loose and unstructured, keeping on staff whom it didn't seem to me did their jobs very well, turning over important ministries to volunteers—and I made sure he knew my views. Gerry had patience, but I managed to deplete his well. Eventually, we stopped speaking to each other.

Then one night, he came to my apartment to celebrate a home Mass for some returning Catholics. Gerry approached me in the kitchen, saying, "I wondered if you might help me with my writing." I knew it was his way of humbling himself as Christ might. That night showed me that avoiding conflict isn't always the answer, that a certain level of self-mortification and acknowledgment of the other's gifts can bring grace into the tensest of situations.

OF GUIDANCE

What's the best way to teach a child to make a snowball—or a birdhouse or cookies or anything else, for that matter? It generally doesn't work well to explain things, step by step, and then sit back and coach (read: criticize) him or her when your instructions aren't followed precisely. Most times, that strategy ends in frustration for everyone. The best way frequently turns out to be getting in there with the child: Make a snowball along with him or her. Help make the birdhouse by assembling the pieces together. Divvy up the measuring of the flour, sugar, chips, and so on. A shared experience is simply more fun... and is a better teacher than direction from afar. Often, that's also the case with adults as well.

The woman of worth knew that too. Some of her servants likely were better at hand spinning than others. Surely, some of them enjoyed it more than others. Her presence showed them all that this was an activity important to the household. I like to think she asked others' advice on whether her yarn was being spun too tightly or loosely... and offered a few valuable tips to those who were struggling with fibers that were breaking, dropped spindles and distaffs, and the like. She would have dealt with their struggles and hers with serenity and encouragement, not with tears of frustration or shouts of annoyance, because she knew true perfection comes only through God.

The woman of worth's confidence was valuable in keeping things in perspective; she showed the servants that this was an important task, and one in which they could take pride, but she also showed them how to regroup and reboot as needed. Because she was with them in the spinning room, they knew her and trusted her. They didn't cower in fear about what would happen when mistakes were made, even though she was the mistress of the house

We can turn to the Blessed Mother as a shining role model for guiding by example. Consider the Presentation: she doesn't weep or challenge Simeon when he warns her that her own soul will be pierced, nor does she press the prophetess Anna for details about her reaction to the baby Jesus. Mary wisely knew the day wasn't about her; instead she pondered in her heart and went about what was required of her as a mother. At the wedding at Cana, she in essence calls on the stewards to follow her example of doing whatever Jesus tells them to do. She is there with her son on the road to crucifixion and at the foot of the cross. In all these cases, people are watching her for her reaction. Every time, she is a model of strength, confidence, and obedience. In sum, Mary shows us how to be fearless, public, and humble in love for her son and, by extension, for those he loves.

A WOMAN OF WORTH

Blessed Elizabeth Canori Mora

1774–1825 • Feast day – February 5

Everyone advised Elizabeth Canori Mora to leave her husband, Christopher. The marriage that had started out with so much promise and so much love had turned into financial ruin and with Christopher taking on a mistress. Even Elizabeth's confessor advised her to seek a legal separation. Today, we would surely support any woman in a similar situation to leave her husband.

Elizabeth gave thought to all the advice she received. But in her situation, she chose to remain married for one simple reason: The Lord had spoken to her, saying, "I desire you not to abandon these three souls, those of your husband and your two children, because I wish them to be saved by your means."[25]

She was humble in her dealings with Christopher. She shared her time and her meager funds and belongings with the poor. One of her daughters remembered, "In the house she applied herself to the lowest and most menial offices...Humility was so dear to her that she practiced without trouble its most heroic acts..."[26] Indeed, as a Secular Trinitarian, Elizabeth's volunteer works included counseling those who, like her, were in troubled marriages.

Nothing, it seemed, would change Christopher's heart, but that did not deter Elizabeth. When he joked about only saying Mass while he was sleeping in his bed, Elizabeth replied, "Laugh as much as you please;

25 Herbert, Mary Elizabeth. *Life of the Venerable Elizabeth Canori Mora* (London: R. Washbourne, 1878), p. 46.

26 Ibid., p. 187.

but after my death you will say Mass, and what is more, you will hear confessions."[27]

Christopher was not with Elizabeth when she died. But it was not long afterward that his own conversion journey began. He spent the final eleven years of his life as a Franciscan priest.

FINDING YOUR WORTH

1. Write a thank-you note to someone whose humility inspires you. It can be anonymous if you prefer.

2. Introduce an activity (cooking, singing, or exercising, for example) at which you're experienced to someone who isn't. Think about how you will guide him or her through the basics so that your joy becomes infectious.

3. Whether it's Lent or not, walk through the Stations of the Cross from Mary's perspective. (There are any number of fine resources available free online, or go with your own thoughts.)

Lord, I thank you for the talents you have bestowed upon me. I ask for the grace to share them with others in a manner pleasing to you and helpful to them.

27 Ibid., p. 216.

CHAPTER 10

OF HANDS *and* ARMS

She reaches out her hands to the poor, and extends her arms to the needy.

Proverbs 31:20

Faith and works: You can't have one without the other. "Demonstrate your faith to me without works, and I will demonstrate my faith to you from my works.... For just as a body without a spirit is dead, so also faith without works is also dead" (James 2:18, 26).

Indeed, Jesus urged those who believed him guilty of blasphemy, "If I do not perform my Father's works, do not believe me; but if I perform them, even if you do not believe me, believe the works, so that you may realize [and understand] that the Father is in me and I am in the Father" (John 10:37–38).

In the same way, when we do the Lord's works, we show our faith to the world. Those we are attempting to help or those who are watching us may not always express gratitude; in fact, we may hear quite the opposite. But we may never know the way our obedience and compassion touch their souls, then or down the road.

For purposes of this discussion, let's look at the woman of worth's reaching out of her hands as active ministry, the kind in which tangible goods and time are offered to the poor. Let's consider her extending her arms to the needy as the kind of compassionate, one-on-one hug that can be even more difficult to provide or receive.

HANDS

"He who labors as he prays lifts his heart to God with his hands," St. Benedict said. Let's pause and think about that beautiful visual image: that as we drive a neighbor to the doctor, shovel a sidewalk, check in customers at the food bank, or greet people at the homeless shelter, we are indeed praying, and that our hands are simultaneously helping others and offering the Lord our hearts. That offering of the money or time to help others at one level is a "debit" against our own self-focused desires. That fifty dollars spent on goods for the parish Giving Tree at Christmas is fifty dollars we can't spend on ourselves or on gifts for those we know and love. The two hours we spend helping shoppers at the food pantry is two hours we'll never get back for sleeping, playing games on our phones, or watching a movie. It's the kind of "debit" the Lord loves, for it's a way of paying forward the goodness he has provided to us.

It's important to emphasize that those debits don't have to involve dollars and cents. Here are a few examples involving some of the corporal works of mercy that show just that type of dual offerings:

- We feed the hungry not only by donating to food drives and charitable organizations, but also by signing up to provide a dinner or two to friends undergoing chemotherapy or other health challenges.
- We shelter the homeless not only by monetary and in-kind donations, but also by advocating for their needs with lawmakers.
- We give alms not only through the parish and diocesan collections, but also by the time we donate to bring together the body of Christ.

Not sure how you want to reach out your hands or bank account? Ask your friends for ideas. You might be surprised at the quiet ways in which they're providing service. I knew a woman for close to a dozen years before I knew she volunteers monthly at a United Methodist church near her home. She's fluent in Spanish and is among the more than four hundred people who gather to provide on-site meals, distribute groceries, conduct health screenings, and the like. I'd seen the line around the church often. I just never knew my friend was one of the people inside.

Two good friends sponsor dozens (yes, dozens) of children each month through a well-known Christian relief service. I didn't learn this from them, but one of their adult children mentioned it in passing. For decades, my friends have lived in the same comfy little house on a major artery. Some people might spend some of that sponsorship money on buying a bigger house on a quieter street. But that's not how these friends roll, nor is bragging about their charitable giving.

Just how far must we reach out our hands? Jesus looked with love at the rich man who wanted eternal life and said, "Go, sell what you have, and give to [the] poor and you will have treasure in heaven; then come, follow me" (Mark 10:21).

Now, in this translation of the Bible, Jesus didn't say we had to sell everything we have. But what about giving half the money you spend each week on coffee, or on wine, or on eating out? What about giving half the amount of time you spend each month on silly online games, or on watching television, or on reading news stories? Yes, it'd be a sacrifice. But if we don't give until it pinches a little, until some part of us dies a little, is it truly giving… or is it a conscience salve?

ARMS

Consider your arms: Are they long, short, muscular, flabby, freckled, hairy? How much weight can you carry, lift, or bench press? When it comes to doing the Lord's work, the physical condition of our arms doesn't really matter. What is important is our willingness to use them compassionately and actively. For when we reach our arms out to others, Jesus embraces us.

There's loads of research into the benefits of touch, including the value of a simple hug. That said, we live in a time and a place where using our arms to physically touch can be tricky, even when our intentions are good. But we can still use them to show compassion in other ways. Again, the spiritual and corporal works of mercy can serve as a guide:

- We touch when we visit the sick or elderly and chat or read aloud or listen.
- We touch when we spend time with the lonely.
- We touch when we go to funeral services or meet with, call, or write an email or note to those who have lost a loved one.
- We touch when we listen to and counsel people who are angry with God and doubt his goodness.
- We touch when we invite someone to join us at Mass.
- We touch when we spell for even thirty minutes a friend who's a caregiver.

Pope Francis extolled what he called "the medicine of caresses"[28] when he met with Italian nurses in February 2018:

> A touch or a smile is full of meaning for a sick person. It's a simple gesture but makes the sick feel accompanied and close to healing, making him feel a person and not just a number.... Remember how Jesus touched the leper: not in a distracted, indifferent, and annoying manner, but attentive and loving, which made him feel respected and cared for.

Now, our efforts to embrace on Christ's behalf won't always meet with a similar embrace. People may not want our listening ear. They may be so

28 https://www.vaticannews.va/en/pope/news/2018-03/pope-francis-audience-italian-nurses-.html

bitter about the hand life has dealt them that they don't want to hear us or spend time with us. They may regard our invitations and offers as just the treacly sort of stuff you'd expect from a "church lady." But you never know how a particular "hug" touches someone's soul. Remember what Jesus said about sowing seeds. Keep reaching out those arms. Don't let them atrophy.

A WOMAN OF WORTH

Saint Katharine Drexel

1858–1955 • Feast day –March 3

Katharine Drexel grew up in the lap of luxury; her father was a wealthy investment banker. But the Drexels raised Katharine and her two sisters with a strong example of true philanthropy. They were generous with their largesse, brought Philadelphia's poor into their home several times a week, and provided financial assistance, clothing, and food. As the girls grew, they helped with serving these guests.

In her twenties, Katharine considered becoming a woman religious, but decided against it, writing: "I hate community life…I'd hate never to be alone. I do not know how I could bear the privations of poverty of the religious life. I have never been deprived of luxuries."[29]

But before she was thirty, Katharine would be deprived of both her beloved stepmother and her father. She and her sisters settled on specific causes they would support with their inheritances, Katharine's selected cause being native Americans. She met with Pope Leo XIII and pleaded for missionaries to the western United States. His response: "Why not, my child, yourself become a missionary?"

29 Walton, Anthony. "The Eye of the Needle: Katharine Drexel," *Notre Dame Magazine*, Autumn 2004.

Why not, indeed? Katharine knew there was a big difference between sacrificing funds... and sacrificing her own lifestyle. But the question stuck with her. When she was thirty-two, Katherine took final vows with the Sisters of the Blessed Sacrament. She spent the next forty-five years establishing schools and missions around the United States.

Katharine's monetary contributions as a woman religious are estimated at $20 million. The value extended to those who received and continue to receive education, encouragement, and other assistance at the Sisters' facilities is priceless.

FINDING YOUR WORTH

1. Consider what you're giving financially to your parish or diocese or a charitable organization. What would you have to give up to increase the amount by five dollars a week? Commit to trying that for a month.

2. How are you reaching out your arms to the needy? How could you find an additional hour—no more—to console or counsel a friend or acquaintance who's starving for some compassion?

3. When Katharine Drexel asked for missionaries, the pope's suggestion that she become one rocked her world. Identify a situation where you have great ideas on how others can be helpful and turn it around to determine what you personally can do to improve things.

Father, show me how you wish me to use my hands, arms, and heart to serve others in your name.

CHAPTER 11

OF CONCERN *and* CONFIDENCE

She is not concerned for her household when it snows—all her charges are doubly clothed.

Proverbs 31:21

Our imaginations are among our greatest gifts from the Lord. All of our lives would be poorer without the music of Mozart, the sculptures of Michelangelo, the paintings of Monet, the words of our saints, philosophers, and others. It's an exhilarating and humbling thing to sit down at a screen or with a piece of paper and see where we're led.

And yet, imagination also can be one of the evil one's favorite places to open up shop in our souls. His residency often begins with two seemingly innocuous words: What if.

- What if my mother doesn't recover from her illness?
- What if I or my children don't get into the right school?
- What if I lose my job?
- What if I never find true love?

Unexpected, unwelcomed events happen to us all. So do unexpected, amazing events. The woman of worth is resilient in her faith during times of adversity and joy. That's not to say she's passive; as we've already seen, she is one active woman! But it is her active relationship with the Lord that keeps her from being overly focused about what might happen here on earth.

CONCERN

Why isn't the woman of worth concerned when it snows? Because she's ready. She's prepared for what is likely to come. In some places, snow in the winter is a given. In others, hot, humid Augusts are unavoidable. In others, hurricanes, tornadoes, wildfires, landslides, earthquakes, and other natural disasters are possibilities. There's no perfect place on this earth, and we do well to prepare ourselves and our families for these potential events. We put together safety plans, we have non-perishable food on hand, we buy generators or batteries. All those precautions are well and good.

Planning relieves or at least alleviates some of our concerns. We run into trouble, however, when we set up our plans as false idols, as insurance that everything's going to go just the way we want, and so we can be complacent. This is the trap "checklist" Catholics fall into:

- Weekly/daily/holy day of obligation Masses attended? Check.
- Tithing done? Check.
- Time outside the abortion clinic or inside the food pantry or homeless shelter or other ministry site done? Check.

What matters is not only our state of readiness, but how we get there. If your hurricane evacuation plan preparation involved a lot of fighting and screaming, the plan may look successful because you and your family escaped with your lives, but was it really? If you are a regular Mass attendee but don't nudge your mind back to the awesomeness at hand when you start to think about what you need to pick up at the grocery store, were you really at Mass? If your tithing doesn't pinch a little, is it enough? If your ministry time is done with a sense of superiority and disdain, you may have done more harm than good for those you serve.

Concern for what might happen is prudent. Obsessing over it or acting in a way that sets everyone else involved on edge is not. Indeed, Jesus chides us for worrying: "Can any of you by worrying add a moment to your life-span? If even the smallest things are beyond your control, why are you anxious about the rest?" (Luke 12:25–26).

We've all heard the saying "Man plans, God laughs." I don't think that's the case. God doesn't upset our little strategies to amuse himself. Rather, I believe his heart is moved with pity because we fail to understand his great love and desire to care for us, if only we would let him. Remember Jesus's words to Martha: "you are anxious and worried about many things. There is need of only one thing. Mary has chosen the better part and it will not be taken from her" (Luke 10:41–42). When we are prudent in our plans and large in our faith, we come closer to the best part of all.

CONFIDENCE

So, we've reined in our futile hope of being completely in charge of our course and have emulated the woman of worth in reasonable preparations for earthly concerns. What's next? Finding the faith and confidence to rely on the Lord. Regardless of how we might mouth sophisms like "Let go and let God," that can be difficult. We know what we have here, good and bad. Predictability is comfortable. Small wonder, then, that St. Augustine observed, "Man, destined to die, labors to avert his dying; and yet man, destined to live for ever, labors not to cease from sinning."[30]

A priest friend once compared our attempts to conceive of heaven and eternity to trying to explain to a baby in the womb what life in the world will be like. All the child knows is a dark, warm, comfortable place. How could he or she even conceive of human touch, noise, good, or evil? In the same way, how can we conceive of heaven, beyond attempting to grasp the idea of unending communion with the Lord?

30 Augustine of Hippo. Marcus Dods, ed. *The Works of Aurelius Augustine, Bishop of Hippo* (Edinburgh: T.&T. Clark), p. 123.

Faith gives us that concept—and that hope that we will be cared for by God after death and are being cared for him today, right now, regardless of how alone we sometimes feel as earthly insults and injuries bombard us. Bask in the comfort Jesus offers us:

- "Are not five sparrows sold for two small coins? Yet not one of them has escaped the notice of God. Even the hairs of your head have all been counted. Do not be afraid. You are worth more than many sparrows" (Luke 12:6–7).
- "Notice the ravens: they do not sow or reap; they have neither storehouse nor barn, yet God feeds them. How much more important are you than birds!" (Luke 12:24).

And so, we as women of worth prepare in the ways within our power. We don't waste time or goods or energy, and we keep the interests and needs of those we love in our arrangements. We also guard against excessive worry, confident in the Lord's love and promises.

In a November 2009 homily, Pope Emeritus Benedict XVI counseled keeping our worldly concerns in perspective, in hope and expectation of what lies ahead:

> We experience in our own journeys that there is no lack of difficulties and problems in this life. There are situations of suffering and of pain, difficult moments to understand and accept. All this, however, acquires worth and meaning if it is considered in the perspective of eternity.... United mysteriously to Christ's passion, we can make of our existence a pleasing offering to the Lord a voluntary sacrifice of love."[31]

31 https://w2.vatican.va/content/benedict-xvi/en/homilies/2009/documents/hf_ben-xvi_hom_20091105_suffragio.html

A WOMAN OF WORTH

Saint Louise de Marillac

1591–1660 • Feast day – March 15

To say Louise's life was a roller coaster would be an understatement. Her parents were not married; she did not know her mother, and while her father, a wealthy French aristocrat, acknowledged her and was involved in her upbringing to a degree, he died when she was twelve. Eventually, she married a secretary to the queen. They were happy together and had a son, but challenges arose again in Louise's thirties; her husband died, as did two uncles, one in prison and the other by public execution.

At loose ends after her husband's death, Louise encountered Vincent de Paul. Vincent agreed to serve as her spiritual director, but with some reluctance as he regarded her as rather self-absorbed and yet another wealthy woman who would be of little use to him in his ministry to the poor. With time, the two established mutual trust and respect and worked together for thirty-five years. Louise's experiences proved to be wonderful preparation for what would become the Daughters of Charity of St. Vincent de Paul. Her time among aristocrats gave her the tact and diplomacy and self-confidence to succeed at fundraising. Her time caring for her husband gave her the skills to train volunteers. Her personal heartaches allowed her to empathize with those in need.

Louise's philosophy on life's ups and downs is one we would do well to embrace: "Changes can and must occur. If they are not accepted, we shall never enjoy the peace of soul that is essential."[32]

32 http://vincentians.com/en/quotes-collection/louise-marillac-quotes/?quotes_page=4

FINDING YOUR WORTH

1. Identify one of your "What ifs." List all the possible outcomes, and how each would impact you spiritually—not your lifestyle or your pride. Consider reassessing the amount of time you spend worrying after reviewing your list.

2. Spend some time with Luke 12, specifically 5–7 and 22–29. Capture the verse that most speaks to you; revisit it each morning and evening in the coming week.

3. Be impulsive in prayer. Add a Rosary or time at adoration or something else you typically don't do. Use the change to be present to God's goodness rather than just rushing through your routine.

Lord, grant me serenity amid the lows and highs of earthly life, confident that you are always at my side.

CHAPTER 12

OF COVERINGS *and* CLOTHING

She makes her own coverlets; fine linen and purple are her clothing.
Proverbs 31:22

My sisters are power users of Pinterest, that addictive website where you can save images and other stuff that inspire you. They both have boards about clothing, bathrooms, seasonal decorations, food, health, and more. The cool thing is that they both have put some of the ideas they've found into action. I, on the other hand, have only twelve items in my For the Home board, and six in my In My Closet board. (My Cool Women Saints board, on the other hand, has 296 pins, but to each her own, right?)

The woman of worth would have had fun with Pinterest and similar tools. I like to think of her exploring new ideas for both her exterior and interior spaces. This is a woman who liked fine things and was discriminating in her tastes.

I envision her home as comfortable—not one that would bowl you over with expensive wall hangings and flooring, but a welcoming place with tasteful touches that create harmony. Her wardrobe was fit for a queen—because of course, she was a daughter of the king.

COVERINGS

English translations of the Bible vary widely on the first part of this verse: coverings of tapestry; coverlets, cushions and rugs; quilts; upholstery; bedspreads; carpets. Universally, however, the focus is on creating a beautiful home, an activity in which the woman of worth is personally engaged.

There's a sense of joy when we make a place ours, whether we're shopping at the local thrift shop or an exclusive high-end boutique. One of my grandmothers spent most of her last thirty years in a series of small apartments. Only one of them had a window in the kitchen. But every time she moved, one of the first things she did was hang a curtain over the sink—to create the feeling she could look outside as she washed dishes. I took a cue from her when I returned to apartment living: a painting of a Norwegian snow scene hangs over my sink.

It's no surprise many translations focus on items we use in our bedrooms since, after all, we spend more than a third of our lives in them. If any room needs to be peaceful and soothing, it's our bedrooms. Creating the bed coverings herself guaranteed the woman of worth that her sheets and quilts and coverlets would have the textures and colors she desired. As she spun and sewed, she smiled at the thought of family members being kept warm during the winter months, when lows would be in the fifties, and cool during the summer heat. We know she pondered all her decisions, so it's lovely to consider her pondering over which colors might work best for this child or another. Perhaps she brought them into the process.

These days, sewing—let's not even get into spinning—is becoming a lost art. A recent study by the British Heart Foundation found that only about forty percent of Britons are confident in their sewing skills, and nearly a quarter doubted even their ability to attach a button.[33] In the

33 https://www.bhf.org.uk/news-from-the-bhf/news-archive/2017/june/bhf-exposes-uk-sewing-skills-shortage-to-launch-the-big-stitch-camapaign

United States, a University of Missouri researcher[34] found that millennials—typically, those born between 1981 and 1996—are much less likely to have mastered sewing of any sort than are their baby boomer parents and grandparents. But lacking those tactical skills doesn't prevent us from creating a sense of spiritual harmony in our homes and communities, nor does a lack of money.

Bed coverings, carpets, rugs, and the rest at their most basic serve to protect something valuable, something we don't want dinged up, dirtied, or marred. In the same way, shared prayer over meals or a family Rosary protect the most valuable thing we have: our faith. So does incorporating the liturgical calendar into our menus. So does focusing our seasonal decorations and practices on the Lord and our cloud of saints rather than on Santa Claus, the Easter Bunny, and Halloween. None of those things is intrinsically bad. But when the gifts under the tree become more important than the gift in the manger and uncovering baskets of candy becomes more important than the rolling away of the stone, we begin to lose the coverings that protect us.

A friend of mine, Meredith Gould, puts it this way in her marvelous book *The Catholic Home*:

> It doesn't matter whether you have four kids or seven cats, Grandma in the upstairs apartment, or single friends within walking distance. You are heir to a venerable structure for creating a Catholic home—the Catholic calendar. Commit to marking time in alignment with the life of Jesus the Christ, and watch your own life be transformed.[35]

34 https://munews.missouri.edu/news-releases/2014/1014-millennials-uneducated-on-important-clothing-care-skills-mu-study-finds/

35 Gould, Meredith. *The Catholic Home: Celebrations and Traditions for Holidays, Feast Days, and Every Day* (New York: Doubleday, 2004), p. 4.

CLOTHING

I had this dress. You've probably had one too. Mine was one hundred percent cotton, short-sleeved, black with little pink and white flowers, some piping on the front, and a tie around the back. It buttoned down the front. It was the type of dress you could wear to Mass, or to work on casual Fridays.

For several years, I was in love with a guy who loved me in that dress; why, I was never exactly clear. We lived about an hour apart, and when I'd tell him about an important meeting I'd had, he'd almost always ask if I'd worn the dress. I wore it often when we saw each other because it made him happy—and made me feel special. Today, he and the dress are no more. But I still have one of the ties to remind me of how attractive I felt when I wore it around him.

Clothing, like coverings, matters. The woman of worth knew that. But rather than an earthly romantic interest, it was God she most desired to please. She dressed in linen rather than wool, the two most common fibers of the time. Linen also was favored for priestly garments, tabernacle materials, and shrouds. It's what King David was wearing when he leaped and danced as the ark of the Lord arrived. In Revelation 19:8, we learn that it was the fabric of choice for the marriage of the Lamb to his bride.

If you wear linen, you know some truths about this fabric. It starts out somewhat stiff and glossy, and softens and whitens the more it's washed. You might compare that with our will; the more we trust in the Lord's love and guidance instead of trying to run things ourselves, the softer and purer we become and the closer we come to righteousness.

Purple was, of course, the color of royalty and priests. The Old Testament is full of references to the use of the color in the tabernacle and the courts of kings. In the gospels, the soldiers put a purple cloak on Jesus along with the crown of thorns to mock him.

The color was prized because it didn't come easily; it wasn't a matter of mixing some herbs or weeds. The hue we know as royal, or Tyrian, purple, came from mollusks. The snail's shell would be cracked and a specific gland removed and dried. It's estimated that 250,000 mollusks were needed for a single ounce of dye.[36]

Why would the woman of worth dress in this color? It seems like a waste of money, an extravagance. But on further reflection, perhaps not. She dressed like the daughter of a king, because that's what she was. Wearing fine linen and purple communicated to all her confidence in herself and her faith in the Lord.

Not all of us can afford linen, and not all of us like the way we look in purple. But regardless of whether we're wearing purple, pink, black, or white; linen, cotton, wool, or a synthetic, we *are* daughters of the king, if we choose to embrace him. One way we show that to the world is how we dress. We eschew garments that show too much cleavage and too much derriere because they show a lack of respect to ourselves, those with whom we interact, and the Lord. We don't overdress to impress or show off our financial success, nor do we ignore our appearance totally. Inside and out, we dress to reflect him.

36 https://www.history.com/news/ask-history/why-is-purple-considered-the-color-of-royalty

A WOMAN OF WORTH

Saint Maria De Mattias

1805–1866 • Feast day – February 4

Appearances were what Maria was about when she was growing up about fifty miles from Rome. It was a very sheltered life, due in no small part to her wealthy parents' fears that she and her siblings would be kidnapped. As a result, the children were not allowed outside to play. Maria passed the hours in front of the mirror, looking at herself and her beauty, in particular her long, blond hair. There was little else to do, since her father opposed teaching reading and writing to girls.

One day when Maria was sixteen, she was engaged in her favorite pastime when her eyes caught an image of the Blessed Virgin. She felt that Mary spoke directly to her, and she began spending more time on her prayer life. The following year, she attended a mission event, and felt called to carry the Lord's message and touch souls in the same way she had heard the priest do. When she was twenty-nine, Maria founded the community now known as the Adorers of the Blood of Christ. In her remaining years, the woman who had found protection by staying indoors and focusing on her beauty traveled on foot or by horseback throughout Italy's small towns and rural areas to establish nearly seventy schools. The woman whose father had opposed her learning the basics of reading and writing saw to it that girls and women would have an education. Clothed in faith and covered in the Lord's love, Maria changed lives, and her community continues to do so today.

FINDING YOUR WORTH

1. What can you do to make your environment at home or at work more pleasing to the Lord, yourself, and others? Think of a change that won't cost money—perhaps rearranging furniture or pictures, playing soft music, or lighting candles at dinner.

2. Ask yourself each day this week what you would wear if you were going to meet Christ at some point. Change your selection as necessary.

3. Identify something about your home or personal appearance that takes up a great deal of space in your brain. Perhaps it's filling your wine cabinet or the time you spend on your hair. Consider how you would redirect the money or time for the Lord if you reduced it by ten percent.

Father, draw this daughter ever closer to you and cover her in your love.

CHAPTER 13

OF SUPPORT *and* SELF-INTEREST

Her husband is prominent at the city gates as he sits with the elders of the land.

Proverbs 31:23

In ancient times, city gates weren't just for protection and monitoring who came in and who went out, although they certainly served that purpose. In peacetime, the gates were also a sort of city hall and courthouse. Those involved weren't formally elected, nor were they paid bureaucrats. Rather, they were the community's wise men, those respected by their peers. That the woman of worth's husband was among that group speaks volumes about him—and about their relationship.

This is the only verse in our study with no direct extolling of the women of worth's virtues. And perhaps that's fitting that there is one. This is a verse of support and self-interest. Like the woman of worth, we know we serve God, not the other way around. We desire that through our efforts, he might be embraced by others. We surrender our own self-interest at the altar and sublimate our own desires to the plan the Lord has for us.

SUPPORT

We know much about the woman of worth's husband from other verses: he has confidence in her; she brings him good; he offers her praise. But in Proverbs 31:23, we see the fruit their union delivers through him. As an elder, he is among those responsible for ensuring their community runs well, that any disputes are settled justly. He can do his job, because he trusts she is doing hers. He values her support, and she doubtless values his. While she was not an elder at the city gates, she was most definitely an elder in the community as well, at home and among her servants, neighbors, and friends.

Traditionally, if the woman of worth and her husband did not know each other before marriage, they would have been introduced to each other to determine whether they thought they were a good match. More than likely, their families would have known each other, or would have had friends in common. What did the woman of worth see when she viewed her future husband and gave her "yes"? Someone whose dreams and goals she shared and could support, and whom she believed would support her in service to the Lord.

A friend of mine was dating two men, and the time had come to deepen her relationship with one or the other. She went to her mother for advice, and the wise lady said, "Choose the one who will help you get to heaven." Three children and more than thirty-five years later, my friend is still married to and in love with the man she chose.

We may start dating someone because there's a spark. We may start up a friendship because our children are in the same activities or because we're in the same professional organizations or because we live in the same apartment building or down the street from each other. But the people with whom we find mutual support in both good and bad times are the ones who help us get to heaven—not necessarily the ones who like our tweets and Facebook and Instagram posts the most or who have the juiciest gossip or the most strokes to our egos.

Support sometimes comes from unexpected or uncomfortable encounters involving the people who appear to be mismatches. It is unlikely we will become lifelong friends with the neighbor who doesn't keep up her yard, the tenant who goes into arrears on rent, or the person at work who is gifted at taking credit for what we and others do. But in those moments, we have a choice: react with love, confident in the Lord's support and direction for us, or react with anger or fear, or retreat into ourselves. Which response gets us to heaven?

The woman of worth's day is full of activity: spinning, shopping, supervising the kitchen, helping the poor, and so many other tasks, all done with wisdom. We get the sense she loves what she does. She is always prepared, always busy, but never frazzled or domineering. She knows the Lord and her husband have her back. They believe in her. Alone, she is nothing. Confident in their support, she can accomplish great things.

SELF-INTEREST

"Mary was a woman *very* interested in making disciples."[37] An acquaintance of mine recently wrote those profound words. The *Catechism* notes just how early she set aside her own self-interest to do so: "By pronouncing her 'fiat' at the Annunciation and giving her consent to the Incarnation, Mary was already collaborating with the whole work her Son was to accomplish. She is mother wherever he is Savior and head of the Mystical Body" (CCC, 973)

Mary's life would have been so much less complicated if she'd said thanks but no thanks to the angel Gabriel. She might have pondered whether she would have additional time with Jesus if her response at the wedding at Cana had been, "What a pity that there's no wine left. Oh well." She might have found it easier to have stayed at home and wept with friends when Jesus was carrying his cross and when he was nailed

37 https://catholicvineyard.com/index.php/2018/04/29/the-collision/?mc_cid=0b42c97e96&mc_eid=6427e28c70

to it. But every time, Mary surrendered and obeyed. "By her complete adherence to the Father's will, to his Son's redemptive work, and to every prompting of the Holy Spirit, the Virgin Mary is the Church's model of faith and charity," the *Catechism* tells us (CCC, 967).

Another New Testament woman was devoted to her sons, but we get a strong sense of self-interest when it comes to the wife of Zebedee. Jesus is on the road to Jerusalem, a trip he knows will not end well; he's just told the Twelve that he will die there. Shortly thereafter, the mother of James and John steps forward and asks that her sons be seated at Jesus's right and left in the kingdom. She must have been bewildered when just days after this exchange, Jesus is persona non grata, headed for a common criminal's death. But then a conversion experience of sorts occurs. Her hopes for earthly prestige for her sons dashed, the wife of Zebedee finds the strength to join Mary near the cross, according to Matthew 27:56. There is nothing to be gained for her sons or herself by this. She is there because she loves Mary and knows Mary needs the comfort of friends.

Discerning the Lord's plan for us can be challenging, especially when we let our egos and self-doubts—for they are really two sides of the same coin—get in the way. We have a desire—secret or otherwise—for public attention, and he calls us to the cloister instead. We are total introverts, most comfortable when we are alone, and he calls us to be teachers. We are uncomfortable around sick people, and we find ourselves as caregivers to a son or daughter with disabilities or a parent in his or her final months. Difficult? Absolutely! Such situations require us to pick up our cross daily and follow. Like John the Baptist, we must decrease our self-centeredness so his presence within us can increase.

A woman named Diane Foley recently spoke in my diocese. She's clearly not someone who relishes the limelight; she used notes at the podium and often forgot to look at the audience. While you may not have heard of Diane Foley, you surely have heard of her son James, a conflict journalist who was beheaded in 2014 in Syria. Today, Diane sets her discomfort aside to advocate for the safe return of American hostages and the rights of journalists in conflict zones. She shares a message of how her faith has sustained her. When I watched the video, I thought of times I have said no or not now to the Lord ... and felt both ashamed of my non-fiat and inspired by Diane Foley's example.

A WOMAN OF WORTH

Saint Thérèse of Lisieux

1873–1897 • Feast day – October 1

Thérèse struggled with self-interest from an early age. How early? Well, there is a not-so-charming story that when she was but two years old, one of her sisters offered a doll dressmaking kit to Thérèse and six-year-old Celine. Celine took a single ball of wool; then Thérèse said, "I choose all," and took the basket and all its remaining contents.

Was it God's will or Thérèse's will when, at fourteen, she took advantage of a papal audience to beg that she be allowed to become a Carmelite, even after a local priest had said she would need to wait until she was twenty-one and the local bishop was mulling the request? Regardless, her temerity is breathtaking. (And, it was not rewarded in the way she had hoped; shortly thereafter, the bishop approved her request, but the mother superior made her wait until three months after her fifteenth birthday.)

In the Carmel, she was no one special. She cleaned, did the laundry, ministered to sick sisters, worked in the sacristy, and supported the community in small, usually unappreciated, ways. Thérèse came to realize that it was her cross and her charism to do the little things, regardless of whether anyone noticed, and to offer that service to the Lord. She was reluctant to take on an assignment to write about her childhood memories. But Thérèse chose surrender and obedience and undertook what would be become *The Story of a Soul*. It was first published in 1898, a year after she died, and has been in print ever since.

FINDING YOUR WORTH

1. It's easy to second-guess people. Why didn't he take the expressway instead of an overland route? Why did she choose that lesser-known local college over the Ivy League university where she was accepted? Resolve that the next time such a situation arises, you will be supportive of the person, even if you disagree with the decision.

2. Identify a "non-fiat" you've given the Lord. What can you do to surrender your self-interest the next time he asks something of you?

3. Spend some time reading about Thérèse of Lisieux's Little Way, either in *The Story of a Soul* or writings about her. Pray with her for the grace to accept and delight in a disagreeable situation.

Lord, grant me the grace to say yes to helping others bring souls to your kingdom.

CHAPTER 14

OF WARES *and* SHARES

She makes garments and sells them, and stocks the merchants with belts.

Proverbs 31:24

Statues of the Blessed Virgin, Thérèse of Lisieux, Teresa of Ávila, Catherine of Siena, Faustina, and other women saints are on shelves in my room. My first-class relic of Maria Goretti is there too. But it's likely the first thing that would catch your eye is the icon I bought from Sister Eliseea Papacioc, a Romanian Orthodox nun. It features the Madonna holding the Christ child, surrounded by images of seven prophets. The golds and reds and greens are vibrant.

I heard Sister speak several years ago about her craft. Soon after she became a novice, she believed writing icons was part of her call. She studied under a noted iconographer, and it took time and care to master the process. In the early days, she made her own paints from local plants and chopped her own wood. The town that is home to her studio has fewer than a thousand people.

It's obvious she loves writing icons; the marketing trips and speeches in the United States and elsewhere, perhaps not as much. But it's part of her call—not only to write beautiful images, but to share them with the world—and so she does it. When we look at this verse, let's consider wares to be the goods, tangible and intangible, the Lord produces through us, and shares to be the means by which we convey them to others.

WARES

Like Sister Eliseea, the woman of worth provided wares of interest to others. Her garments and belts likely were not the sort we'd find at our favorite department or specialty store, virtual or bricks and mortar. Scholars seem to agree that the items may have referred to priestly garb; think of the "belt" as the fascia sash or band cincture we see Catholic priests wear with cassocks today (indeed, it is still referred to as a belt in some countries). Some translations use the word girdle rather than belt in this verse, which brings to mind the spiritual armor passage of Ephesians (specifically, "stand fast with your loins girded in truth" (Ephesians 6:14).

Girdles in the woman of worth's time also would have referred to the ribbons, leathers of fabric that held flowing desert garments in place. This could be an analogy to the order God brings to otherwise unrestricted lives. If you've tried to live without him or without rules, you know the peace and relief that comes when chaos ends.

Sometimes, our wares aren't as tangible as Sister Eliseea's icons or the woman of worth's garments and belts. For example, our offerings may include serving as cantors, ushers, extraordinary ministers, or lectors. We may be amazing cooks, seamstresses, or decorators. We may be gifted at facilitating Bible study sessions or leading the parish council. We all have gifts of some sort, and it's important that we recognize them, offer gratitude to the Lord, and look for opportunities to develop them to the fullest. Being lazy with our gifts, regardless of our skill level, dishonors them.

Being best is irrelevant to developing our wares. Creating or enhancing them brings us joy, and honors God. If we love baking cookies with our children, it doesn't matter that we don't make them as well as our mother did. If we enjoy web design but aren't confident of our skills, ministries currently without a website may be thrilled to be the place we can learn to improve. Remember the parable of the talents in Matthew 25? The servant who received a single coin buried it rather than investing it in the world. When the master returned, he was angered that nothing had been done with this gift, and ordered that the servant be thrown into darkness.

The woman of worth has no fear about being cast into darkness like the servant. She recognizes her gifts and invests in them so that they might do much good. They are keys in her evangelization toolbox, the ways in which she carries the Lord's Good News in forms we can see, hear, feel, taste, and touch.

SHARES

All three of the synoptic gospels share Jesus's simile of light. My favorite version is Luke's: "No one who lights a lamp hides it away or places it [under a bushel basket], but on a lampstand so that those who enter might see the light" (Luke 11:33). All the talents and skills with which we are blessed are worthless unless we share them.

Consider some of the ways in which your spiritual life has been enriched. Maybe it's through the written word, the reflections or memoirs of the Doctors of our Church, or authors of today such as Father Jacques Philippe, Scott Hahn, Elizabeth Scalia, Peter Kreeft, or Joan Chittister. Maybe it's through movies and videos, such as those from Bishop Robert Barron. Maybe it's gazing at paintings or sculptures of key sacramental or religious events, including Michelangelo's "Pietà." Think about how your life would have been diminished if those people had yawned and said, "Thanks but no thanks, God. Writing/painting/sculpting is a lot of work with little financial reward. I don't think I'm going there."

Then consider the times you've been thanked for what in your mind is simply being obedient to the Lord. (Honestly, I don't think obedience is ever simple, but hear me out, all right?) Maybe it's watching your adult daughter or son parent with love and gentleness and when you compliment her or him, one day, the response is, "I learned that from you." Maybe it's when a friend comes to you with a thorny problem and says, "You're the only one I knew would listen." Just as great artists do what they do to glorify God, so do you glorify him when you share the gifts of the Holy Spirit: wisdom, understanding, counsel, fortitude, knowledge, piety, and fear of the Lord. You don't have to be perfect at sharing; you just have to have the courage to let him work through you.

Marketing our wares isn't necessarily about buying a social media ad or handing out flyers and brochures. We market our wares in each encounter we have every day, with the Lord, with family members, with friends, with colleagues, with people we see on the street or in the grocery store. Let's not waste a single "transaction."

A WOMAN OF WORTH

Saint Catherine of Bologna

1413–1463 • Feast day – March 9

Literally, Catherine was a Renaissance woman, given the time in which she lived. She was also a renaissance woman in terms of her gifts and how she shared them.

Born into an aristocratic family, Catherine spent her early years at court. When she was barely a teenager, Catherine discerned that was not the life she was meant to live and became a Franciscan tertiary. By the time she was nineteen, Catherine and some friends had founded a Poor Clares monastery in her hometown of Ferrara; later, she would establish a second monastery in Bologna.

We don't often think of women religious as artists in the traditional sense. But that, Catherine was. Her painting of St. Ursula can be seen in a Venetian gallery. Her prayer book, including her illuminations, or miniatures, once was owned by a pope. She played the viola.

She wrote a 5,000-line poem about Jesus's life. But Catherine is best known for her work *Seven Spiritual Weapons Necessary for Spiritual Warfare*, which provided guidance to her novices and detailed some of her visions, heavenly and demonic.

However, Catherine did not spend all her time in such obvious creative pursuits. She served stints as abbess, though she did not particularly care to. At the Ferrara monastery, she also served as a laundress, a baker, and as caretaker for the community's animals.

Catherine's embrace of whatever task the Lord set before her inspires us to say yes with the same gratitude and humility to activities we might not enjoy as much, but that are needed by the body of Christ.

FINDING YOUR WORTH

1. Make a list of three things you do well. If you have trouble coming up with gifts, ask a family member or friend to weigh in. What can you do to improve your skills and reflect Christ more transparently?

2. Make a list of three people whose gifts have inspired you. The gifts may be tangible or intangible; the people may be well known or not, alive or dead. Write a note or prayer of thanksgiving that shares how your spiritual life was deepened by them.

3. Set aside an hour in the coming week to spend time appreciating beauty. Consider going to a museum, concert, or park, or perhaps spending an hour at an adoration chapel. Thank the Lord for this and all his goodnesses.

Lord, I delight in the light you place in my path through the sacrifice of others. Help me to be a beacon for you as well.

CHAPTER 15

OF CONFIDENCE *and* DIGNITY

She is clothed with strength and dignity, and laughs at the days to come.

Proverbs 31:25

It seemed to come almost out of nowhere in the fall of 2017, the #metoo movement that battles environments of sexual assault and harassment. Almost every woman I knew had a story about date rape, a boss who propositioned her, an acquaintance who aggressively put his hands where they shouldn't have been put without permission.

Such violations aren't unique to the twenty-first century. We find a number of similar incidents in the Bible:

- Tamar is raped by her half-brother Amnon (2 Samuel 13);
- Dinah is raped by Shechem (Genesis 34:2);
- Lot's two virgin daughters are offered to the Sodom townsmen in place of the visiting angels (Genesis 19:8);
- Bathsheba, the wife of a soldier, is seen bathing by David, the king, who desires her (2 Samuel 11:4). Was the balance of power such that sex between them could have been consensual?

But just as today, not every man in biblical times objectified women. Indeed, in his 1995 *Letter to Women,* St. John Paul II cast Jesus as our champion: "Transcending the established norms of his own culture, Jesus treated women with openness, respect, acceptance and tenderness. In this way he honored the dignity which women have always possessed according to God's plan and in his love."[38] How much of his message has been heeded, the pope acknowledged, is a matter of debate.

The woman of worth wore her strength and dignity like armor. There may have been people who envied her or started rumors about her or wished her ill. But she moved about her community with confidence that she was doing the Lord's work and had no reason to worry about the future.

OF CONFIDENCE

How do we find the confidence we need to defend ourselves against the slings and arrows the world fires at us? Indeed, the *Catechism* advises us *not* to rely on our own strength, but on Christ's promises and "the help of the grace of the Holy Spirit" (CCC, 1817).

Consider the way Jesus conducted himself during his Passion. Consider the way our holy martyrs went to their deaths: with eyes on the Lord and the hope of eternal life and with compassion and forgiveness for those who persecute us. Indeed, as Jesus told us in the Sermon on the Mount: "Blessed are you when they insult you and persecute you and utter every kind of evil against you [falsely] because of me. Rejoice and be glad, for your reward will be great in heaven. Thus they persecuted the prophets who were before you" (Matthew 5:11–12).

Sometimes, the attack comes not from others, but from within. We don't believe we're good enough or strong enough for the work the Lord has laid before us. Or, we don't believe he can really do anything about

38 https://w2.vatican.va/content/john-paul-ii/en/letters/1995/documents/hf_jp-ii_let_29061995_women.html

it anyway. A sizable minority of Catholics (28 percent) surveyed in December 2017 by the Pew Research Center said they didn't believe in God as described in the Bible; 69 percent said they did. (Another 2 percent who identified as Catholic said they do not believe in God or a higher power of any kind.) Perhaps even more puzzling, among U.S. Christians, Catholics ranked last in their belief in God or a higher power as all loving (88 percent), all knowing (78 percent), or as being all loving, all knowing, and all powerful (61 percent).[39]

If you don't believe, it's more difficult, though not impossible, for God to give you strength of the sort he gave the Old Testament's Judith. She had been a widow for more than three years, maintaining the household her husband had left her. When she heard the people and their leaders were prepared to surrender to an enemy force, she felt the call to leadership. Before initiating her plan for victory (gaining the trust of the opposing general and decapitating him), she prays for strength: "Your strength is not in numbers, nor does your might depend upon the powerful. But you are God of the lowly, helper of little account, supporter of the weak, protector of those in despair, savior of those without hope" (Judith 9:11).

Not surprisingly, the plan works, the city rejoices, Judith gives thanks, and Israel is saved.

And, as women of worth, when we are confident in the Lord and the strength he provides, we truly can laugh at the days to come, for nothing the world throws at us can diminish us.

OF DIGNITY

It was not all of the woman of worth's successes with spinning and sewing and trading and planting that brought her dignity; she always had it. Dictionaries tell us that dignity is a sense of self-respect, of being worthy of honor or respect. Dr. Donna Hicks of Harvard University's Weatherhead

39 http://www.pewforum.org/2018/04/25/when-americans-say-they-believe-in-god-what-do-they-mean/

Center for International Affairs and the author of *Dignity: The Essential Role It Plays in Resolving Conflict,* writes: "Dignity is our inherent value and worth as human beings; everyone is born with it."[40]

The *Catechism* is eloquent on the dignity of the human person, saying it "is rooted in his creation in the image and likeness of God" (CCC, 1700). St. John Paul II in his *Centesimus annus* explained that "beyond the rights which man acquires by his own work, there exist rights which do not correspond to any work he performs, but which flow from his essential dignity as a person."[41]

In the same way, our dignity can't be stolen. Did Jesus lose his dignity when he was paraded through Jerusalem, bent and bloody, mocked and jeered at? Absolutely not. Does a young woman who's been given a drug, raped, and left for dead near a garbage can lose her dignity? Absolutely not. Does the child who sees a perpetrator coming for yet another round of cruelty lose his or her dignity? Absolutely not. The only way we can lose our dignity is if we willingly give it up by a sinful life, interior or exterior. And even in those cases, if we throw ourselves on the Father's mercy, we can regain it (CCC, 1700).

40 https://www.psychologytoday.com/blog/dignity/201304/what-is-the-real-meaning-dignity-0

41 http://w2.vatican.va/content/john-paul-ii/en/encyclicals/documents/hf_jp-ii_enc_01051991_centesimus-annus.html

A WOMAN OF WORTH

Saint Teresa of Ávila

1515–1582 • Feast day – October 15

The Catholic Church's first female Doctor (teacher) learned early not to rely on things of the earth for her strength. Her beloved mother died when Teresa was just fourteen years old. At twenty, she entered the local Carmelite convent, and within two years the robust young woman became extremely ill with what may have been malaria, falling into a coma for four days and becoming paralyzed for three years. She would never regain all of her physical strength.

Teresa lacked spiritual strength in this period as well. She enjoyed the convent's social life, with much frivolousness and time spent entertaining the wealthy donors who supported the community. It took years—in her writings, she is frank about the lack of a true prayer life until she was forty—but Teresa began to reconsider the appropriateness of the lack of discipline within the convent. Her reform, backed by the pope, to bring the Carmelites back to their roots of absolute poverty and useful work began in 1562. Not everyone welcomed this back-to-the-basics approach; at one point, Teresa was ordered to retire and stop founding new convents. She obeyed, then returned to her ministry when the order was lifted. All told, her strength and God-given dignity resulted in the establishment of sixteen convents in twenty years...and some of the church's most profound writings about prayer.

FINDING YOUR WORTH

1. Select a favorite image of Mary. For example, you may like a window at your parish that depicts the Annunciation, or looking at a pietà may move you to tears. Make some notes about Mary's strength in that bewildering, joyful, or sorrowful scene.

2. We sometimes fail to respect the dignity of family members or friends by teasing them a little too much or raising our voice with them even though they are not the cause of our anger. Do something—an apology, a note of gratitude, or other action—for someone you have disrespected in this way.

3. Is there a situation, current or from the past, that is threatening to sap your strength? Spend some time today with one of Teresa of Ávila's best-known prayers:

> Let nothing disturb you; nothing frighten you. All things are passing. God never changes. Patience obtains all things. Nothing is wanting to him who possesses God. God alone suffices.

Lord, I ask for the strength to treat all I encounter today with respect for their human dignity, even when they do not respect mine.

CHAPTER 16

OF WISDOM *and* INSTRUCTION

She opens her mouth in wisdom; kindly instruction is on her tongue.
Proverbs 31:26

We need only look to the Book of Proverbs' opening lines to begin studying this verse: "Fear of the Lord is the beginning of knowledge; fools despise wisdom and discipline" (Proverbs 1:7).

When we embrace fear of the Lord, that's not about cowering in a corner, scared to death of his judgment today, tomorrow, and on the final day. It's also not about scrupulosity, a problem I struggle with at times. (Was it six or seven weeks since my last confession? What if there's a sin I forgot to confess? But I digress ...)

Fear of the Lord is about gratitude, respect, homage, humility, and a whole lot of other words that are beautiful to hear but can be so difficult to do. Fear of the Lord in some ways begins with accepting that God is God, that we are not, and that while we are on earth, we can never begin to understand all his desires and ways and plans.

The woman of worth chooses her words carefully. The wisdom she obtains by study and prayer gives her the depth needed to instruct. She also is unafraid to provide loving correction where appropriate. When the woman of worth talks, people listen—and learn.

WISDOM

In *The Catholic Catechism: A Contemporary Catechism of the Teachings of the Catholic Church,* Servant of God John A. Hardon, SJ, explained wisdom this way: "Where faith is a simple knowledge of the articles of belief that Christianity proposes, wisdom goes on to a certain divine contemplation of the truths that the articles contain, that faith accepts without further development."[42] For example, as Catholics, we believe in Jesus's true presence in the consecrated host and wine. In faith, we accept that teaching; we're not required to attempt to understand how it happens. In wisdom, we contemplate Jesus's gift in feeding us in such an intimate way. We are humbled by the giving up of his body and blood so that we might live with him in eternity.

Father Hardon puts it even more simply and beautifully in the *Catholic Dictionary*: "Wisdom means knowledge that is so perfect it directs the will to obey God's commands."[43]

Who among us doesn't yearn for, doesn't strive for, that sort of knowledge, where our will and the Lord's are in complete harmony? Who doesn't have a few holy moments when that has happened? In early 2018, I went to a retreat center intending to spend a weekend praying about the next steps for a women's conference. The other three partners had had to leave the endeavor. I knew God wanted the event to continue, but we'd lost a substantial amount by holding the event at hotels, and it was more money than I could afford to lose by myself.

And yet—when I got to the center, I forgot about my prayer intention. I read some books. I interacted with other retreatants. I prayed for others' intentions. I caught up on my sleep. Then all of a sudden, Sunday morning

42 Hardon, John A. *The Catholic Catechism: A Contemporary Catechism of the Teachings of the Catholic Church* (New York: Doubleday, 1981), p. 201.

43 Hardon, John A. *Catholic Dictionary: An Abridged and Updated Edition of Modern Catholic Dictionary* (New York: Image Books, 1980), pp. 533–534.

came, and I realized I had never talked with God about this. I offered him some praise and thanks for all he had done to spark and continue this little ministry, then humbly asked for his desire. Within a few minutes, a voice spoke the name of my parish, which, coincidentally, has a large center. Within a month, my pastor had signed off on the plan.

Now, God doesn't speak out loud to me often, and maybe he doesn't to you either. But if we have the courage and, yes, wisdom, to trust in him and accept his will, he'll generally make it quite clear to us in some way. And if you don't know what that wisdom looks like, read Ecclesiastes 8:1: "Wisdom illumines the face and transforms a grim countenance."

Wisdom doesn't need to know why bad things happen to good people, where Jesus was between the time he was put into the tomb and before the resurrection, or how the Holy Spirit impregnated Mary. Wisdom accepts the Father's will and power and contemplates how it displays his awesome love for us. The woman of worth opens her mouth to help others join her in that contemplation.

INSTRUCTION

Just as wisdom is accepting in faith and contemplating the mystery of God's great gifts and love, instruction is about communicating that wisdom to others. Wisdom is talking the talk internally, deeper and richer as time goes on. Instruction is being able to show that wisdom to others so that they too may become wise. Think of it this way: Wisdom is knowing how to ride a bike. Instruction is teaching someone else to do it.

In writing, there's this saying: Show, don't tell. That means don't write that someone was angry. Instead, show the person's face turning red, his fist clenching, her voice moving up an octave. Jesus did a whole lot of showing—remember the wedding at Cana, the miracle of the loaves and fishes, and the raising of the synagogue ruler's little girl? Even when Jesus is teaching, he tells stories that show action, often with dialogue. That's how he did his best work: face to face, friend to friend, engaging people at their own level.

Think about the teachers you've had, inside the classroom or out in the world. Who taught you more: the friend who seemed to have unending patience when she taught you to knit, even though you're righthanded and she's lefthanded, or the friend who told you that you'd "just know" when the egg whites were stiff, except you didn't and so your meringue effort was an epic fail? Who taught you more: the second-grade teacher who stayed after school with you sounding out your vocabulary words, or the fourth-grade teacher who took away recess for the entire class for a week because she was sure someone had stolen something from her desk? It's all instruction, but sometimes it teaches us something other than the intended lesson.

It works the same way with spiritual works of mercy, most of which involve instruction. Which is more likely to bear fruit:

- Telling an adult son who has announced he's an atheist that he's going to hell, or talking about the ways in which your faith has challenged you and brought you comfort?
- Telling a friend who's been out of work for a year that he needs to downsize his lifestyle and you're not going to give him money anymore, or compiling a list of resources for low-income people and offering to help him see for which he qualifies?
- Telling a friend you can't stand to be around her anymore because she's always so negative, or gently stopping her when the familiar tapes start to play and asking what needs to change to improve her feelings, if not the situation?

For the woman of worth, "kindly" is always part of her mode of instruction. She skillfully navigates the line between judgment and education. She doesn't back away from difficult conversations but approaches them after prayer. She knows, as a former boss of mine used to say, you can say anything to anyone; it's all in the way you say it.

The woman of worth also knows when her part is complete with those who turn away her offer of instruction. Part of wisdom is recognizing when conversations become toxic, and not putting our own salvation in danger. In his final instruction in Romans, St. Paul counseled, "[I] urge you, brothers, to watch out for those who create dissensions and obstacles, in opposition to the teaching that you have learned; avoid them" (Romans 16:17).

Indeed, Jesus's final instruction when he sends forth the Twelve is also good instruction for us: "Whoever will not receive you or listen to your words—go outside that house or town and shake the dust from your feet" (Matthew 10:14).

A WOMAN OF WORTH

Saint Hildegard of Bingen

1098–1179 • Feast day – September 17

Tradition has it that Hildegard was the tenth child born to her parents, and so she was "tithed" to the church. She may have been as young as eight when she went to live with the anchoress Jutta, who provided Hildegard with instruction on the Psalms and possibly taught her to read and write. The enclosure began drawing other young women, and by the time Jutta died in 1136, a Benedictine community had developed. Upon Jutta's death, Hildegard became abbess, a position she would hold for the rest of her life.

That Hildegard possessed wisdom and "brilliant intelligence," as Pope Benedict XVI put it, is beyond question. *Scivias* ("Know the Ways"), her three-volume set of visionary theological writings, impressed the sitting pope so much that he encouraged her to write more. And so she did—a morality play, music, poems, medical and scientific documents, and even a new alphabet.

Her gift of instruction was equally impressive. Hildegard undertook several preaching journeys.[44] She provided advice and counsel to at least one king as well as bishops and priests. She continues to instruct Catholics and others today as a Doctor (teacher) of the Church. In bestowing that title on her in 2012, Pope Benedict XVI noted that, "above all (she) maintained a great and faithful love for Christ and the Church."[45]

FINDING YOUR WORTH

1. Do you have a list of things you plan to ask God about if you get to heaven? This might include why a loved one was taken away from you, or why you suffer with a chronic illness. Pray for the wisdom to see past the questions that seem so important, and to use that time you usually spend in bitterness, resentment, and confusion to contemplate the mysteries of our faith.

2. Sign up to teach religious education, a Bible study session, or other activity at your parish that will require you to instruct others. Don't fret about whether you're smart enough. Just give it a try.

3. Does a family member or friend come to you often for help with the same problem? Maybe it's a financial shortfall; maybe it's a pattern of selecting the wrong friends. Pray for the words to provide correction in a loving manner.

**Lord, bless me with the desire for wisdom,
so that I might grow in love for you,
and with the words to use when called
to instruct others in your name.**

44 http://w2.vatican.va/content/benedict-xvi/en/apost_letters/documents/hf_ben-xvi_apl_20121007_ildegarda-bingen.html

45 http://w2.vatican.va/content/benedict-xvi/en/homilies/2012/documents/hf_ben-xvi_hom_20121007_apertura-sinodo.html

CHAPTER 17

OF DILIGENCE *and* LEISURE

She watches over the affairs of her household, and does not eat the bread of idleness.

Proverbs 31:27

It came on the television screen just before the late-night news: "It's 10 o'clock. Do you know where your children are?" And even as a child, I somehow felt safer that yes, my mom knew exactly where we all were, even later when we were teenagers and out on dates or at sporting events or slumber parties. Even more importantly, she *cared* where we were.

Watching over a household's affairs is no easy task, whether you're living with a large family on forty acres in the country, with a spouse or roommate in a posh urban condo, or by yourself in a cozy home in the suburbs. Stuff breaks and needs to be fixed or replaced. Rooms need to be cleaned. Groceries need to be bought. People need to get to work, to school, and other commitments on time. The activities never seem to end, and even when you get a routine down, something changes. On the rare day that everything gets done, the temptation is to relax with mindless entertainment because, after all, you've earned it.

The woman of worth takes her cue from the way God manages his household—with love and care, with plenty of time for leisure, which is not the same as idleness. Leisure is her place to rest in the Lord and to contemplate where he desires her to go and how.

DILIGENCE

The woman of worth watches over the affairs of her household with diligence; and let's be honest: diligence is not very exciting.

Diligence is the woman who cleans up after the party instead of letting the dishes go until the next morning. Diligence is the woman who says no to free tickets to the theater or a sporting event she loves because it's a holy day of obligation and she needs to go to evening Mass. Diligence is the woman who is there every week for Bible study, even when the lesson didn't excite her and someone else in the group is working her last nerve.

Diligence is faith that's warm—not cold and not a roaring fire that burns out. It's the sown seed that takes root. Diligence, boring as it may be, is the counter to acedia or sloth, which looks a lot like spiritual discouragement, burnout, or boredom.

And it just may be the key to staying on the narrow path to salvation.

We live in a world where people expect to be entertained constantly, where pedestrians have died because they were so busy on their phones that they didn't look up before they crossed the street. We're easily bored, and after a while, nothing can be as boring as religion and ritual and obligation.

But as women of worth, we also know that nothing can be as exhilarating and exciting and challenging as religion and ritual and obligation. Every single sacramental event is an opportunity for holiness in action, shared or viewed, a gift that at times can move us to tears in awe and wonder when we stop to think about what is happening. Every single time we wake a child or help bag groceries at a food pantry, it can feel like a sacrament too.

We need diligence for those other times, when it feels like we're just going through the motions, because going through the motions is better than not going through the motions.

"Do not neglect the gift you have," the letter writer advises Timothy. "Be diligent in these matters, be absorbed in them, so that your progress may be evident to everyone" (1 Timothy 4:15). It's good advice. Effective evangelization doesn't have to be showy, with larger than life theatrics and witnesses. Sometimes, it can just be letting people see that you continue to show up and trust in the Lord's plan, boring as it may seem at times.

LEISURE

When I was a young reporter, a journalist from a rival news organization was working on an investigative piece on illegal gambling during the fall hunting season, and a scoop fell into his lap when he found two top elected state officials in a bar engaged in, you guessed it, illegal gambling. When the men saw the reporter, one asked, "Are you off duty too?" Of course he wasn't—nor were they. Everyone in the state heard about what happened, and the officials both paid fines.

As Christians, we're never off duty either. But that does not mean we never get time to rest. Remember, even God did that on the seventh day.

I've always been a bit leery, and perhaps a bit afraid, of idleness. I can't tell you the last time I took more than a day or two off completely from my day job and my writing and editing side jobs. I sandwich quarterly lunches or dinners with a rotation of friends in between other appointments. It's the rare week that I'm at home more than two evenings. I tell you all this not to impress you with how valued I am by others, but to admit how little I value myself. And that spills over into how low a priority I put on setting aside leisure time with God. I rationalize that it's all right to be writing on Sundays, since it's generally Catholic "stuff," and to binge-read the Bible study group assignments for the week.

But more than a decade of operating at that pace has begun to take its toll. I don't write or edit as quickly or efficiently as I did even a couple years ago. So about a year ago, I joined an adoration team at my parish, and once a month from 9 to 10 PM. on Thursdays, I sit and adore. Just sit and adore. No reading, no formulated praying, no prayer intentions of others until the end. It's only an hour a month, but it's a start, in addition to the fifteen minutes I always spend before Sunday Mass.

My friend Letitia is a big proponent of observing the Sabbath, even if all you can manage initially is an hour or so. For years, she's opted to schedule few social events on Sundays, take a walk, and change up her weekday spiritual readings. She also puts together "Sunday soup" in the slow cooker, something that's now been a family tradition for decades because it's low-stress and low-maintenance.

Like me, Letitia is not someone who naturally does idleness well. Her example helps me to begin to understand that while we desperately need leisure time with the Lord, we are never idle in helping to bring souls to his kingdom, but we will fail at that mission without some time to recharge and breathe in his goodness.

A WOMAN OF WORTH

Saint Monica

c. 331–387 • Feast day – August 27

Monica's life is a shining light of faith-filled industriousness and diligence. While she was raised as a Christian, her parents chose for her husband a man named Patricius, a town councilor who also happened to be a pagan. The marriage was marked both by his infidelity and violent temper and Monica's charity even amid difficult financial times and her devotion to Christ.

Monica was patient with Patricius and never stopped praying for him. He became a Christian the year before he died, and Monica also had the joy of seeing the conversion of her difficult mother-in-law. Her two younger children by all accounts were faithful Christians; her daughter would go on to shepherd a community of women religious.

The oldest, Augustine, as we all know, was a different story. The family scrimped and saved to give him the education his intellect merited, but the young man was less than diligent in his studies. In his late teens, he acquired a live-in girlfriend, and they proceeded to have a son. He took up Manichaeism, a non-Christian theology that considered God to be less than omnipotent. Disgusted, Monica refused to open her home to Augustine after he completed his studies.

Soon thereafter, Monica's tactics changed. Augustine left for a teaching position in Rome, and she followed. (He was less than forthright about his sailing plans, so Monica ended up on a different voyage.) She arrived in Rome only to learn he had gone on to Milan. And so, she followed. There, Augustine encountered the bishop, Ambrose, and was impressed with his intellect. Ambrose became Monica's spiritual adviser, and together they provided the intellect and example that resulted in

Augustine's conversion seventeen years after his journey began. Monica died about six months later.

FINDING YOUR WORTH

1. Where is diligence lacking in your faith practice? What non-onerous routine could you establish to embrace diligence?

2. Make a date with God. Spend at least thirty minutes this week with him at leisure, with no competing thoughts or electronics.

3. Pray for someone whom you've nagged, begged, and cajoled to no avail about going to church or confession.

Lord, following you at times can be a bit of a slog. Help me to appreciate the beauty of routine and to accept its rhythm.

CHAPTER 18

OF MOTHERING *and* EXCELLENCE

Her children rise up and call her blessed; her husband, too, praises her: "Many are the women of proven worth, but you have excelled them all."

Proverbs 31:28–29

The people who know us best love us best. Our family members and best friends may joke with us about our shortcomings, such as our inability to start the day without an iced venti decaf skinny mocha. They may admonish us with love about our propensity to gossip and other behaviors that threaten our souls. But through it all, they know our worth, because they have seen it time and again, under the most difficult and challenging of situations.

What is family these days? Many of us are blessed to have our parents, children, and siblings all living close enough to pop over for an impromptu cup of coffee or to join us for a dance recital or a soccer match. For others, family is our parish community or a body of friends who love and support us. Regardless, it all starts with the Lord.

"All the love God has in himself, all the beauty God has in himself, all the truth God has in himself, he entrusts to the family," Pope Francis said at

2015's prayer vigil for the Festival of Families.[46] "A family is truly a family when it is capable of opening its arms to receive all that love."

The woman of worth was blessed indeed by her family's awareness of the gifts she bestowed upon them in the Lord's name. She mothered them and provided an example of excellence.

MOTHERING

The woman of worth's children may be children no more; after all, it's noted that they "rise up," which may be a reference to growing up. They've seen her their whole lives, attending to their physical, emotional, and spiritual needs. But since no woman is perfect, they also saw those moments when she was frustrated with them, their father, other members of the household, and herself. There had to be times she was tempted to lash out in anger or fear. But even then, those who called her mother—regardless of how they came to that situation—learned from the way she mastered her emotions and surrendered to what the Lord desired of her.

The model for us all when it comes to surrender and mothering is, of course, the Blessed Virgin. In *Walking with Mary: A Biblical Journey from Nazareth to the Cross,* Edward Sri lays down the stakes Mary faces when the angel Gabriel greets her:

> She is being called to stand in the tradition of Israelite heroes like Moses, Joshua, David, and Jeremiah—people who suffered, sacrificed, and gave themselves radically for the Lord. She is now being called to a daunting mission that will involve many challenges and hardships, and the future of God's people will depend on how she responds. No wonder the Bible tells us that Mary felt "greatly troubled" when she heard these words![47]

46 https://w2.vatican.va/content/francesco/en/speeches/2015/september/documents/papa-francesco_20150926_usa-festa-famiglie.html

47 Sri, Edward. *Walking with Mary: A Biblical Journey from Nazareth to the Cross* (New York: Image, 2013), p. 41.

And yet, she says yes. The *Catechism* tells us: "By pronouncing her 'fiat' at the Annunciation and giving her consent to the Incarnation, Mary was already collaborating with the whole work her Son was to accomplish" (CCC, 973).

We all have the opportunity to say yes to Christ every single solitary day: in the way we deal with unpleasant situations, in the way we interact with people we find difficult to love, in the way we react when the evil one seeks room in our souls. We can obey those two greatest commandments, or we can react with less than love for the Lord, his people, and ourselves. We can always return to God's good graces through the sacrament of penance and reconciliation when we confess with a contrite spirit. But we don't know what the lingering effect might be on those who were affected by or saw our bad behavior. Certainly, something to ponder in our hearts as we struggle to think before we act or speak rashly.

St. John Paul II acknowledged our special role in his 1995 letter to women, which includes thanks to all mothers, wives, daughters, sisters, workers, and those in the consecrated life: "In giving themselves to others each day women fulfill their deepest vocation. Perhaps more than men, women *acknowledge the person,* because they see persons with their hearts"[48] (emphasis original).

EXCELLENCE

The women of worth's husband has seen her, up close and in person, as wife, mother, household manager, businesswoman. He isn't actually comparing her, act by act, word by word, with their friends and acquaintances, for he doesn't know them as intimately. For her unique role in the world, there is no one better in his eyes.

What would the woman of worth's response be to his beautiful compliment? I don't think she would have diminished it by saying some of the things we find ourselves saying when we are praised:

48 https://w2.vatican.va/content/john-paul-ii/en/letters/1995/documents/hf_jp-ii_let_29061995_women.html

- "Me? I'm not so special. What about our neighbor/my sister/your colleague? I can't hold a candle to them."
- "You're forgetting about that day that I didn't do/did XXX."
- "Living with you gives me a whole lot of practice when it comes to forgiving and serving—just kidding!"

More likely, she thanked him, and gave some credit to him and to God.

What woman does not spend at least a few seconds each day comparing herself with someone else, generally to her own detriment? We're not as thin as a celebrity whose work we enjoy. We don't sing as well as a Grammy-winning artist. We're not as smart as the woman who leads our Bible study. We don't cook as well as our mothers. The list goes on and on. And life is no easier when we sit in judgment and determine we are the best hostess in our circle of friends, the best lector in the parish, or the fastest woman in our age bracket in the half marathon, because we know that someone else is going to surpass us sooner or later. Try as we might, we're not perfect.

You can point to Scripture for what we perceive as a requirement for perfection: "So be perfect, just as your heavenly Father is perfect" (Matthew 5:48). But Luke's take is subtly but importantly different: "Be *merciful*, just as [also] your Father is merciful" (Luke 6:36, emphasis added). God's grace and our willingness to receive it bring us closer to him and to perfection. We will not achieve it on earth. He loves us despite—or perhaps because of—our flaws and struggles, for the more we look to him to be free of them, the more bound to him we become.

"God is the first to love," Pope Francis said in a June 2017 audience. "God does not love because there is something in us that engenders love. God loves us because he himself *is love*, and, by its very nature, love tends to spread and give itself. God does not even condition his benevolence on our conversion. If anything, this is a consequence of God's love"[49] (emphasis original).

Think of God as the woman of worth's husband. He sees us, he knows us in ways no one else can. And as hard as we may be on ourselves, he knows we are worthy.

A WOMAN OF WORTH

Blessed Maria Corsini Quattrocchi

1884–1965 • Feast day – November 25

There have always been lay couples who were saints, starting with Joseph and Mary. In some cases, entire families—generally with wealth or power—were canonized in a time when the process was less formal. There's a certain grace, then, that the first couple to be formally beatified together lived very ordinary, upper-middle-class lives in twentieth-century Rome.

Maria Corsini and Luigi Beltrame Quattrocchi were married on November 25, 1905, and had three children in the next four years. Luigi worked for the government and in the financial sector; Maria was a writer and volunteer nurse. They both were active in a number of faith-based organizations. A fourth pregnancy proved problematic, but Maria carried the baby to term.

Life wasn't always easy in ways we might find familiar. Luigi, who going into the marriage was not as devoted to the Lord as Maria, suffered a dark night of the soul. His smoking was a source of annoyance for Maria, as

49 https://w2.vatican.va/content/francesco/en/audiences/2017/documents/papa-francesco_20170614_udienza-generale.html

was his travel for work. Still, as St. John Paul II put it at their beatification: "Among the joys and anxieties of a normal family, they knew how to live an *extraordinarily rich spiritual life*"[50] (emphasis added).

The Quattrocchis are indeed noteworthy for their piety—a nightly family Rosary, First Friday holy hours, a Sacred Heart image on the mantel, retreats, and so on. Maria and Luigi both became Third Order Franciscans. But the family celebrated the Lord in everyday life as well, including getaways to the mountains and seashore and sports. "We brought them up in the faith, so that they might know and love God,"[51] Maria wrote.

FINDING YOUR WORTH:

1. Mother someone today with grace and joy. It can be someone in your family, a friend, or someone you don't know who needs your help for a matter of minutes.

2. Make a list of at least three things about you that God loves. Put it in your purse or wallet for reflection when you feel unloved.

3. Spend some time with Luke 6:36. Where is the Lord calling you to show mercy so that you may be perfected?

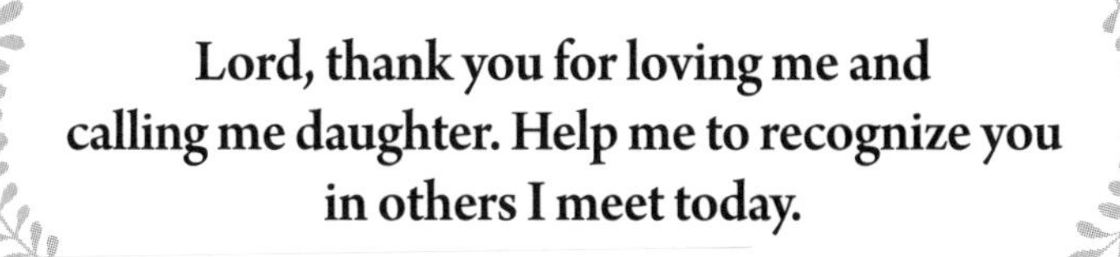

Lord, thank you for loving me and calling me daughter. Help me to recognize you in others I meet today.

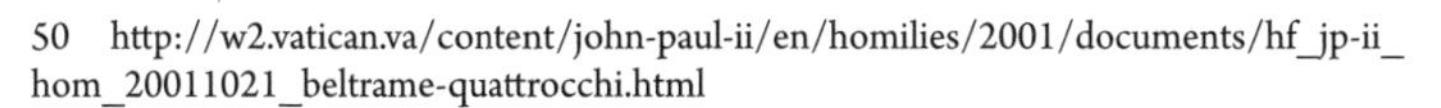

50 http://w2.vatican.va/content/john-paul-ii/en/homilies/2001/documents/hf_jp-ii_hom_20011021_beltrame-quattrocchi.html

51 http://w2.vatican.va/content/john-paul-ii/en/homilies/2001/documents/hf_jp-ii_hom_20011021_beltrame-quattrocchi.html

CHAPTER 19

OF CHARM *and* TRUE BEAUTY

Charm is deceptive and beauty fleeting; the woman who fears the LORD is to be praised.
Proverbs 31:30

When I was young, I was sure there was a secret word. If only someone would share it with me, I would be short instead of tall, thin instead of fat. My hair would be curly instead of straight, and I would be able to keep my mouth shut rather than blurting out one-liners that seemed funny in the moment but hurt people deeply. I would be a cheerleader or on the drill team instead of on the debate team and the school newspaper.

It took me a long time, but I finally figured out that word, and it turned out it wasn't a secret at all. It was Jesus. He loves us whether we're a size two or size twenty-two, and he loves us in spite of our worst moments. His example and guidance can bring true charm and beauty into our lives, regardless of what the world sees or doesn't see in us.

CHARM

What's wrong with a little charm? It makes us feel good to be around charming people. They "get" us. They sympathize with us. They make us believe that in that particular moment, we're the most important, special thing in the world to them. When we think of charm, we think of world leaders, television personalities, family members, colleagues. They tend to be leaders in at least one aspect of life. One in particular comes to mind for me. He was a senior executive, with a lot of people in his chain of command. He had risen up through the ranks and worked hundreds of miles from our headquarters. Jeff had a way of greeting you, whether it was in a meeting or in a chance encounter in the hallway, as if seeing you was the best thing that had happened all day. It didn't matter whether you too were a rising star, a worker bee, or a slacker. It didn't matter whether Jeff remembered your name, either. You got the dazzling smile, the warm handshake, the few seconds as the center of his orbit. He's a good man; none of the welcome was fake, and it also didn't prevent him from being tough when he needed to be.

But charm misused can wreck havoc with our souls. Remember the serpent and Eve? Remember Delilah and Samson? It's one of the evil one's favorite weapons, to gull us into believing that we truly are important to the person we barely know, and that he or she has no ulterior motive for the praises they heap on us.

You might contend that Jesus is the most charming person who's ever walked the earth. There was just something about him that people warmed to. Think of the way that Andrew and John, who had been disciples of John the Baptist, began following Jesus after hearing John the Baptist call him the Lamb of God. Andrew's following begat Peter's. Even Nathanael, who expressed doubt to his friend Philip that Jesus could be the Messiah—that changed when he talked with Jesus.

Jesus drew crowds when he was teaching and preaching, and even when he was trying to pray. Young and old, Jew and Gentile, almost everyone wanted to be around him. That is, unless you were a Pharisee or a scribe or until things got difficult to understand or scary, like when Jesus talked about the Eucharist or when his raising of Lazarus gave the authorities the ammunition they needed to arrest him. His charm didn't count for much when Judas betrayed him or Peter denied him.

Was Jesus's charm fleeting? No, because his message was constant. Regardless of to whom he was speaking or the circumstances, he gave comfort, but he spoke the truth—kindly, yes, but clearly and unswervingly. He called out the evil one when he appeared, rather than attempting to woo him. During his time in the desert, he battled the devil's temptation with the most effective weapon ever: Scripture. Small wonder that the devil went to look for someone weaker on whom to ply his trade.

Our charm is fleeting only when we use it insincerely, as a means to obtain what we want, rather than loving the person and seeing the face of Christ in him or her. Used wisely, charm can be a healing balm for those we know and even those we don't. That kind of charm is what the Lord desires from us.

TRUE BEAUTY

Quick, who's the most beautiful woman you've ever seen? You'll be forgiven if you say Beyoncé, Angelina Jolie, or someone else in popular culture from today or yesterday. Women who rely solely on their physical beauty, however, have a short shelf life in our world. There's always someone younger, someone better proportioned, someone with more perfect features waiting to step up. (And perhaps that is why both Beyoncé and Angelina Jolie have so many fans, because their public image isn't limited to their beauty.)

How about a five-foot Albanian nun who had a big nose and a crooked smile? How about your own mother or a person who was like a mother to you, who cleaned your scrapes, delighted in your accomplishments, and consoled you during your disappointments? How about the woman in a wheelchair who greets you by name each week at Mass, even though you're embarrassed to admit you don't remember hers? How about the friend who escaped an abusive marriage in another country, fleeing with nothing but the clothes on her back and her infant son in her arms? How about the image of Mary, holding the broken, dead body of her son?

"Women are uniquely endowed with gifts of receptivity, generosity, sensitivity, and maternity," Pat Gohn writes in *Blessed, Beautiful and Bodacious: Celebrating the Gift of Catholic Womanhood*. "When we trust these things, we become beautiful from the inside out.... When we exercise our gifts, beauty always emerges."[52]

Women of worth see true beauty in the way those around them witness to the Lord in their service and their surrender to him. They know that that beauty doesn't come out of a bottle or under a surgeon's knife. It comes from within, when we are brave enough to let him go to work.

A WOMAN OF WORTH

Blessed Agnes Phila

1909–1940 • Feast day – December 26

If you put Agnes Phila's name in an online search engine, you'll find a picture of a broad-faced, stern young Thai sister whom you probably would not want to cross. To me, it's the face of one of the most beautiful, challenging martyrs of the twentieth century.

Agnes was nineteen when she took her final vows with the Congregation of the Lovers of the Cross in Laos. She returned to her native land as a teacher in 1932. As time went on, Thailand became more and more unfriendly to westerners and to Christianity.

Agnes and another sister continued teaching and speaking out publicly for their faith, even after the Songkhon parish priest was deported and a local catechist was executed in mid-December. On Christmas Day, the police chief came to meet with the sisters, and said that if they con-

52 Gohn, Pat. *Blessed, Beautiful and Bodacious: Celebrating the Gift of Catholic Womanhood* (Notre Dame, IN: Ave Maria Press), p. 10.

tinued to talk about God, they would be killed. Coolly, Agnes asked if he had enough bullets to kill all Christians. He assured her he did. She asked if their gun barrels were sufficiently oiled.

The next day, the police chief received a letter from Agnes—and a vial of gunbarrel oil. In the letter, Agnes said the women, their cook, and three teenagers were ready to die. "Please open the door of heaven to us so that we can confirm that outside the religion of Christ no one can go to heaven....We will be thankful to you and will be grateful to you for it. And on the last day we will see each other face to face."[53] The women were executed later that day.

Agnes's example shows us that true, pure beauty comes from within, and from faith and confidence in the Savior and his love.

FINDING YOUR WORTH

1. Each time you pass a mirror today, take thirty seconds to say an Our Father. End by thanking the Lord for finding delight in you.

2. Spend some time viewing artists' renditions of the Blessed Virgin at various stages of her life—the Annunciation, the Visitation, the Presentation at the Temple, and so on. Where do you find beauty in these depictions?

3. Attempt not to comment on someone's appearance, attractive or otherwise, today. Offer compliments instead on the way she or he handles a difficult situation or interacts with someone in a respectful manner.

Lord, help me to see the beauty you find in me ...and in those I find difficult to love.

53 Suphannahong, Sheba. *Frontier Towns on the Mekong*, p. 49. 2013. EBookIt.com.

CHAPTER 20

OF PRAISE *and* GLORY

Acclaim her for the work of her hands, and let her deeds praise her at the city gates.

Proverbs 31:31

Sound the trumpets! Signal the choirs of angels! The woman of worth's work is done. In verses 31:10–30, we learned much about this woman—her strength, her industriousness, her wisdom, her skills. Now comes the time for her to put down the distaff and spindle and to go to the place where her true worth will be celebrated and rewarded forever.

PRAISE

We already know the woman of worth's husband and children believe she is a treasure, and we can reasonably infer that the servants respect and admire her. Why then the need for praise at the city gates? Perhaps it was a matter of earthly legacy: those who love her think all should know about her great gifts. Think about it: aren't there times that the Lord's goodness is so apparent that you want to shout it from the rooftops? Maybe it was the day your first child was born, or maybe when what seemed to be a death sentence of a diagnosis turned out on further examination to be wrong? It wasn't enough to tell everyone you know; the whole world needed to be in on the news.

I suspect the woman of worth smiled a little at the others' desire to make her front-page news—and then kept on doing what she'd always done, serving God and her community. She knows the praise that matters most comes from God.

As women, we tend to be people pleasers. We avoid conflict and run from disharmony. We'll do our best to make everyone happy, even if that means making three different dinners at three different times or buying three different kinds of toothpaste for our family. We'll run ourselves ragged, skip meals (or eat twice), and forgo a rare unscheduled Saturday if we can satisfy someone else.

The woman of worth likes happy people too. But she's not going to sacrifice her God-given responsibilities to do so. With her, he always comes first, and sometimes that means people will be disappointed in her. She doesn't stay up nights trying to figure out how to change that. His praise and his grace are more than sufficient for her.

GLORY

"I believe in one God, the Father almighty, maker of heaven and earth, of all things visible and invisible." We say it at every Mass. Pretty amazing stuff. But why did he do it? "God created the world to show forth and communicate his glory," the *Catechism* tells us, "that his creatures should share in his truth, goodness and beauty—this is the glory for which God created them" (CCC, 319).

That, the woman of worth has done. She has lived God's truth in her interactions with others. She has shown his goodness in the way she interacts with her husband, her children, her servants, the poor and needy, and her trading partners. Her appreciation for God's beauty has been displayed by the attention she provides to her vineyard, her spinning, and her handiwork.

This woman was seen as an almost impossible standard centuries ago. We regard her as the same today. And yet, there are bits and pieces of her in all of us. Coming closer to that standard also brings us closer to the Lord, and time is running out for each of us.

"For I am already being poured out like a libation, and the time of my departure is at hand," the writer tells Timothy. "I have competed well; I have finished the race; I have kept the faith. From now on the crown of righteousness awaits me..." (2 Timothy 4:6–8).

May we be found to be, like the woman of worth, good and faithful servants, when we close our eyes one last time.

A WOMAN OF WORTH

Saint Catherine Labouré

1806–1876 • Feast day – November 28

The story goes that when Catherine's mother died, the nine-year-old kissed a statue of Mary and said, "Now, dear lady, you are to be my mother."[54] It was the start of a beautiful relationship.

Catherine was a novice with the Daughters of Charity of St. Vincent de Paul when Mary first appeared to her, saying the Lord had a mission for her. About four months later, the Blessed Virgin returned, giving her specific instructions for a medal to be created based on a model that showed Mary standing on a globe, crushing a serpent's head. Catherine dutifully shared the information with her confessor. It took him two years to act—initially, he doubted the young nun—but in 1832, the first two thousand copies were struck of what would be known as the Miraculous Medal. Within four years, millions had been sold.

54 http://www.amm.org/aboutamm/story%20of%20st%20catherine.aspx

By that time, however, Catherine had all but disappeared from view. She moved from working in the kitchen to the laundry, then to overseeing a poor farm for elderly men. It was not until shortly before her death—forty-six years after the apparitions—that Catherine revealed to her superior that she, not her confessor, had been originally given the Miraculous Medal assignment and that Mary had freed her from her silence. Catherine died confident in knowing she had fulfilled her part of the mission.

FINDING YOUR WORTH

1. Revisit Proverbs 31:10–30. Which verse and its ideals seem the furthest away from your daily life? What spiritual aids might bring you closer to achieving it?

2. Write a one-paragraph eulogy for yourself. Consider using words from the woman of worth verses. Or, if you know who you want to give your eulogy, ask that person to do this; then sit down and discuss it together.

3. Get creative! Draw a picture, sing a song, or write a short poem or prayer giving the glory to God for your gifts and how you can't wait to thank him in person.

Gracious Father, help me to keep my eyes ever focused on you, your Son, and the Holy Spirit in the time remaining on my earthly journey. Believe that I desire nothing more than to see you, face to face, in heaven.